Charles Darwin

Published by

MAPLE PRESS PRIVATE LIMITED
Corporate & Editorial Office
A 63, Sector 58, Noida 201 301, U.P., India
phone: +91 120 455 3581, 455 3583
email: info@maplepress.co.in, website: www.maplepress.co.in

2024 Copyright © Maple Press Private Limited

Printed in 2026
India

ISBN: 978-81-19898-20-6

23 22 21 20 19 18 17 16 15 14

Charles Robert Darwin, the English naturalist, biologist and geologist, was born in 1809. He was known for his "Theory of Evolution" and was interested in natural history even when he was just eight years old.

After his basic education, he joined the University of Edinburgh Medical School with his brother Erasmus in 1825. But very soon, he found the subject boring and neglected his studies. Annoyed by his attitude, his father sent him to Christ's College, Cambridge, to pursue a Bachelor's degree in Arts, which would make him eligible to become an Anglican country parson.

It was during his stay at Cambridge that he got acquainted with Professor Henslow, who had a great knowledge of botany, entomology, chemistry, mineralogy and geology. This was the friendship that influenced Charles throughout his career!

Henslow persuaded Charles to study geology. Therefore, he joined Professor Adam Sedgwick's geology course.

In 1831, when Sedgwick planned to visit North Wales for an investigation of older rocks, he recommended that Charles accompany him. That tour taught him how to determine the geology of a country.

The actual turning point in Darwin's life, however, occurred after he returned from the tour, and he spent five years aboard the Royal Navy exploring ship HMS Beagle.

He received a letter from Henslow that read: "Captain FitzRoy of the Beagle is willing to accommodate any young volunteer to go with him as a naturalist on the voyage of the 'Beagle' without pay. I suggest you take this opportunity to be the volunteer."

Charles was eager to accept the offer. But when he told his father about the same, his father raised an objection, saying, "Charles! If you can find any man of common sense who advises you to go, I will give my consent!" At once, Charles wrote back to Henslow, refusing the offer.

The next morning, he went out as usual for his shooting expedition when his uncle Josiah Wedgwood called him and said, "Charles! I came to know about your new offer for the Beagle voyage. Quite interesting... I hope you are wise enough to accept it!"

Charles hesitantly said, "No, indeed! I had to refuse. Father says it is insensible to accept it!"

"Oh, really? Hmm… I see. Come; I will drive you over to your place. Let me talk to your dad about that!"

His uncle discussed the advantages with Charles' father and convinced him to allow Charles to proceed with the voyage.

On his part, Charles, who had been extravagant while in Cambridge, assured, "Father! I know it is not going to fetch me any income, and I should depend on you for expenditures during this journey. But, trust me, I am clever enough not to spend more than my allowance on board the Beagle!"

Charles' father said with a smile, "Oh, that's good! People tell me you are very clever!"

The voyage was finalised, and Charles set sail on December 27, 1831. That voyage turned out to be the most important event in his life and even determined his entire career. Charles found it to be the real training and education of his learning.

For the next five years, Charles would correlate whatever he had thought or read earlier with whatever he saw and experienced about natural science. He collected rocks, fossil bones, shells, etc., and made detailed notes about the animals, plants and geology of the countries he visited along the way.

His observations during the voyage made him ponder how new species evolved.

He started working on his idea in 1838. In 1858, 20 years later, he concluded that all living species descended from a common ancestor and that the branching pattern of evolution (the changing or developing) is a result of the process of natural selection. He introduced this theory of "natural selection" in a joint publication with Alfred Russel Wallace, another naturalist, explorer and anthropologist who held the same views. In 1859, Charles incorporated these ideas and propounded the theory of evolution in his book *On the Origin of Species by Means of Natural Selection.*

Charles Darwin presented his scientific theory with evidence of the similarities between humans and other mammals.

Initially, his views shocked the world, as at the time, it was widely believed by people that all living beings on Earth had been created by one "Creator," God! Darwin's book challenged this "truth" mentioned in the book of "Genesis."

By the 1870s, however, a great majority
of the educated people and the scientific
community had accepted his idea of
"evolution" as a fact.

As Alfred Russel Wallace put it, Darwin
had "wrought a greater revolution in human
thought within a quarter of a century than
any man of our time–or perhaps any time."

Darwin's findings on human evolution bring together the whole gamut of life sciences and remain the basis for all the new and upcoming theories about the diversity of life on Earth. His legacy continues to intrigue us and the generations to follow.

World Scientists

CHARLES DARWIN

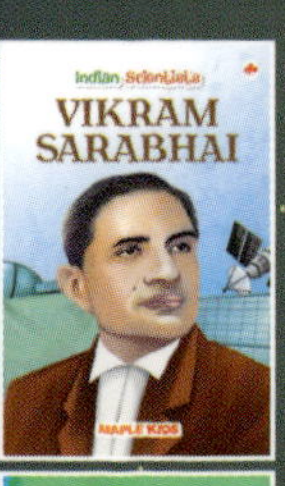

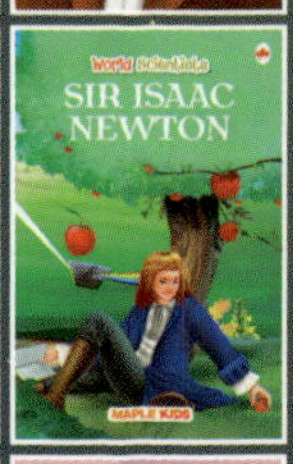

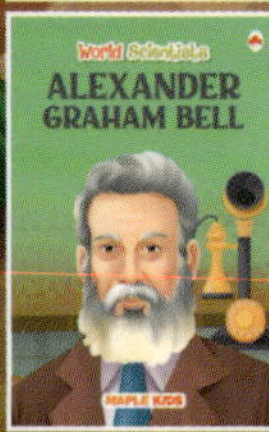

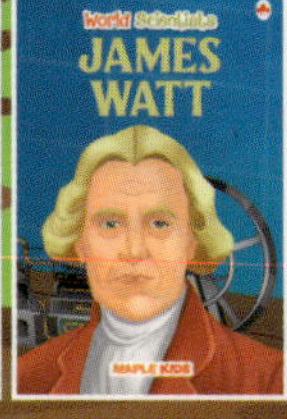

children

catalogue

e-book available

C. V. RAMAN

C. V. Raman

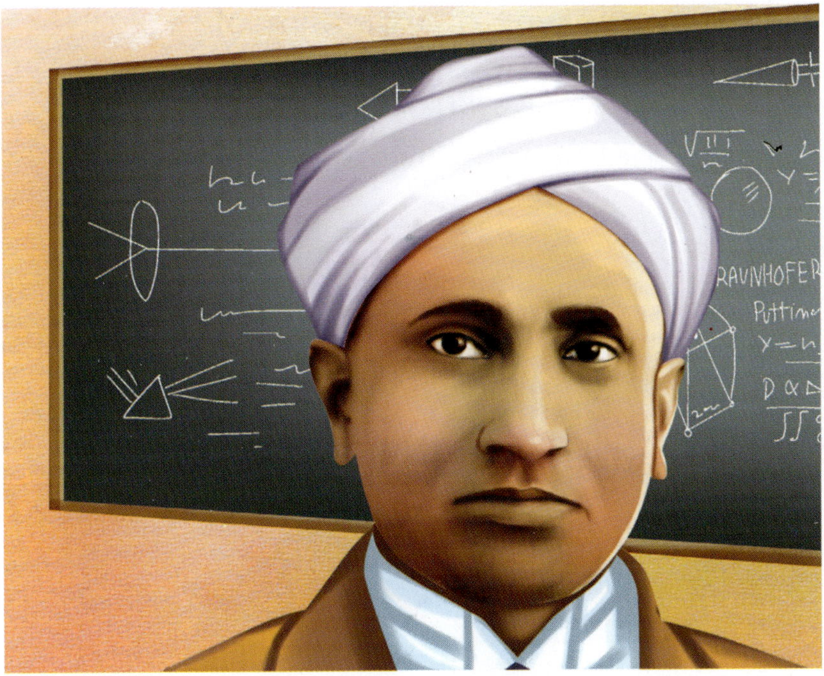

Published by

MAPLE PRESS PRIVATE LIMITED
Corporate & Editorial Office
A 63, Sector 58, Noida 201 301, U.P., India
phone: +91 120 455 3581, 455 3583
email: info@maplepress.co.in, website: www.maplepress.co.in

Printed in 2026
India

ISBN: 978-93-95976-96-1

32 31 30 29 28 27 26 25 24 23

Sir Chandrashekhar Venkat Raman was born in 1888 in Tiruchirapalli of Tamil Nadu, to Chandrashekhar and Parvathi.

His father was a professor of Mathematics and also a music lover, which meant that the household had a balance between academia and melody.

Raman studied at St Aloysius Anglo-Indian High School in Vishakhapatnam. He turned out to be a gifted student as he completed his matriculation at the age of 11. He became the youngest B.A. graduate with a gold medal in Physics and English from Presidency College, Madras, at 16. By 1907, he had completed his M.A. from the same university and earned the highest rank.

He was interested in physics, but at the time, science didn't have many career opportunities. Therefore, to earn a living, he qualified for the Indian Finance Service and was posted as an Assistant Accountant General in Calcutta. Despite having such a reputable job, he was not content with his choice of career.

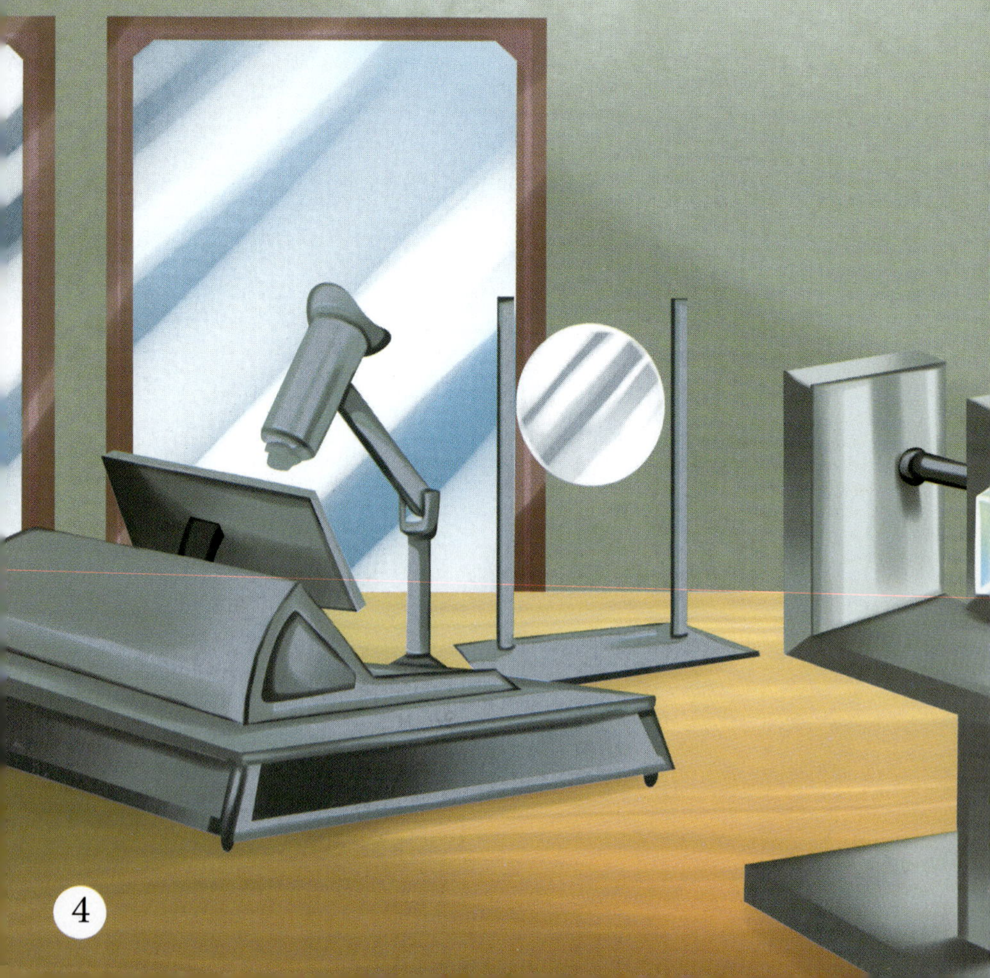

He soon joined the Indian Association for the Cultivation of Science in Calcutta. IACS was a research institute established that offered scientists a space to research various topics; however, it had not published any research articles till then.

Raman started his research right after joining, and his work on Newton's Rings in Polarised Light became the first article from the institute to be published in *Nature* – a renowned British weekly scientific journal which is still in circulation.

Slowly and steadily, Raman established his presence as a researcher in Physics and attracted more attention in India as well as abroad. He was also in touch with Lord Rayleigh, who discovered the phenomenon of the scattering of light. Rayleigh addressed Raman as a professor and even invited him to London to research alongside him. Since Raman's health was always sensitive, he couldn't have survived England's harsh weather and stayed in India.

In 1914, the University of Calcutta chose
Raman to become a Palit Professor of
Physics, but due to the First World War,
his appointment was delayed. However,
the University started sending all students
to research under Raman, and they
were always inspired by his knowledge.
Finally, in 1917, Raman started as a full-
time professor at the Rajabazar
Science College and quit his job
as a civil servant.

Soon, his work started gaining more recognition, and in 1921, he was invited to London to deliver a lecture. While the trip to London was eventful, the trip back home became a historic one. During his return journey, he kept admiring the vibrant blue colour of the Mediterranean Sea.

Standing beside another traveller on the ship, Raman said, "How beautiful is this blue of the sea? Mesmerising!"

The fellow traveller said, "Indeed, it is beautiful. I wonder what makes it so blue."

"Well," Raman said with a look of confusion. "They say it's a reflection of the sky's colour…"

"Oh! Makes sense," the man nodded. Raman said, "I don't think so, though. Look at the sky."

"It is blue, isn't it?" the man said.

"That it is. But look at the water again," Raman said, and they looked at the water.

"And the water is still blue," the man shrugged.

"Do you observe that there's a difference? The sky is a lighter hue; the sea is a deeper and more vibrant hue. If the latter is merely a reflection, how come it's a different shade?"

The man was at a loss for words, and Raman
knew there was more to this phenomenon
than the given explanation. Upon returning
home, he started researching this odd
scattering of light and found out that his
assumptions were true - the colour of the
sea wasn't the reflection of the sky.

This discovery made in the field of
scattering of light came to be known as
the Raman Effect.

In 1930, C. V. Raman became the first Indian to receive the Nobel Prize in the field of Science. The Indian Government acknowledged his work by bestowing upon him the Bharat Ratna.

He dedicated his entire life to Physics and continued researching until his last breath in 1970.

C. V. Raman showed the world that all one needs is a thirst for knowledge and the desire to do something great.

Indian Scientists

C. V. RAMAN

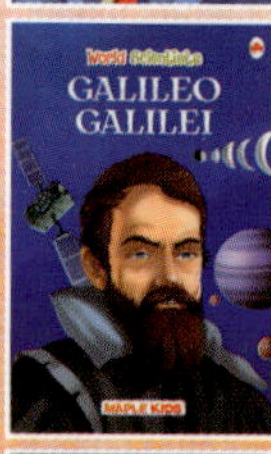

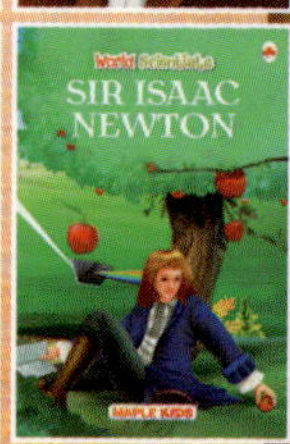

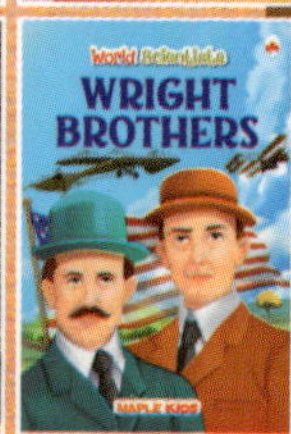

children

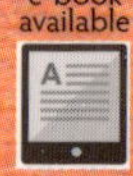

World Scientists
GALILEO GALILEI 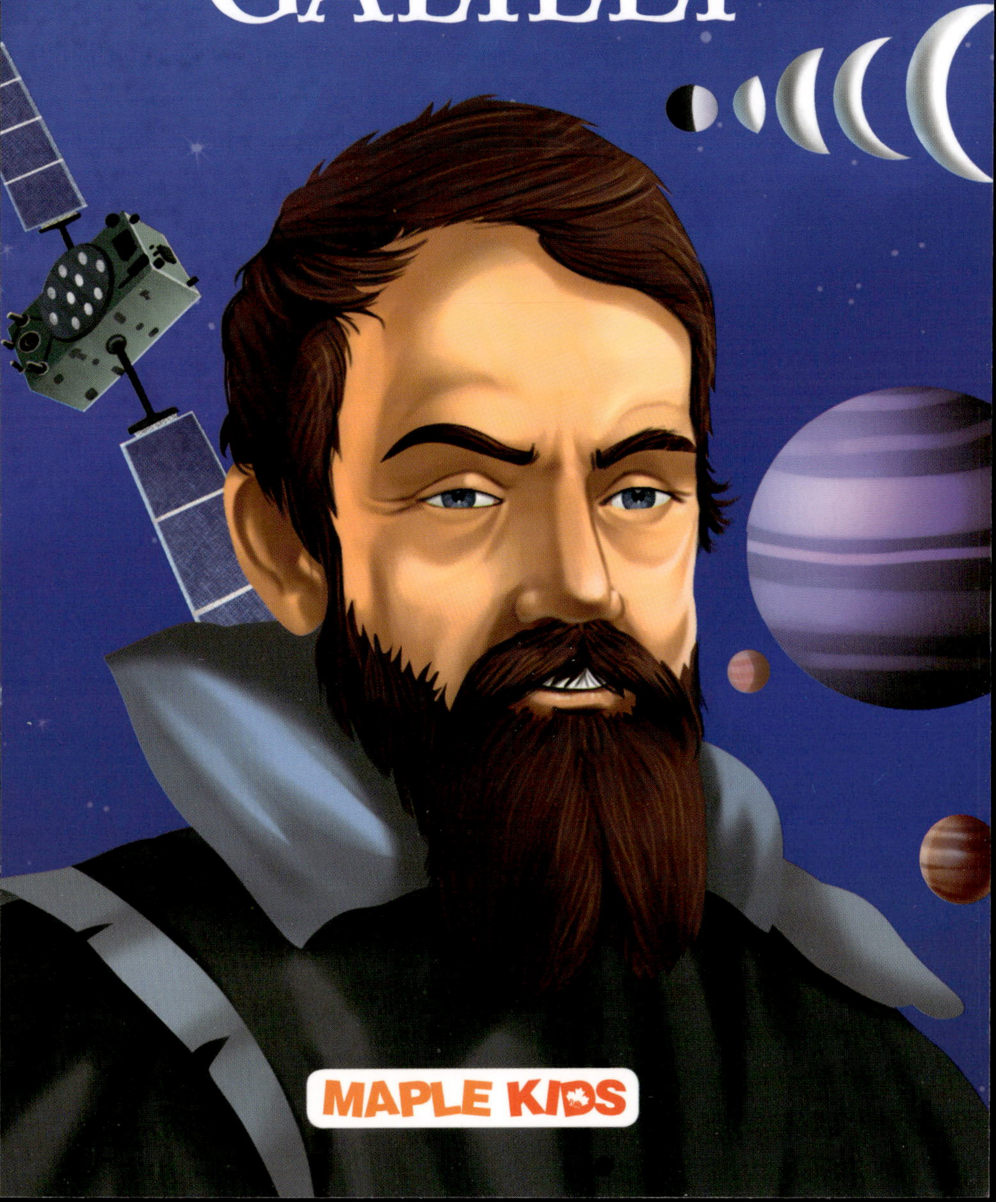
Maple Kids

Galileo Galilei

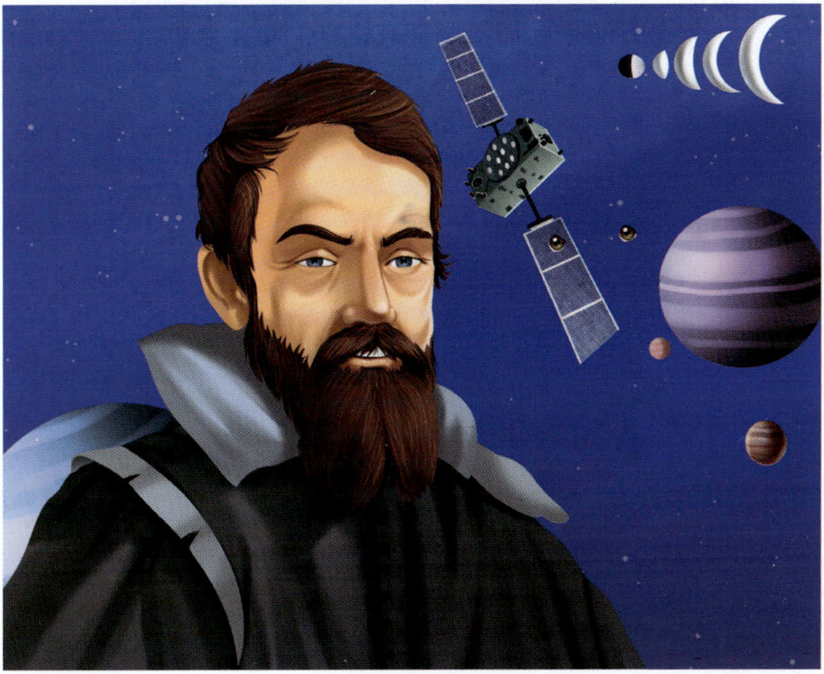

Published by

MAPLE PRESS PRIVATE LIMITED
Corporate & Editorial Office
A.63, Sector 58, Noida 201 301, U.P., India
phone: +91 120 455 3581, 455 3583
email: info@maplepress.co.in, website: www.maplepress.co.in

Printed in 2026
India

ISBN: 978-81-19898-02-2

23 22 21 20 19 18 17 16 15 14

Galileo Galilei, popularly known as the "Father of Modern Science," was born on February 15, 1564, in Pisa, Italy. After his basic education, his father enrolled him at the University of Pisa for a medical degree. In 1581, he attended the lectures of Girolamo Borro, the Italian philosopher, and that created a spark in him.

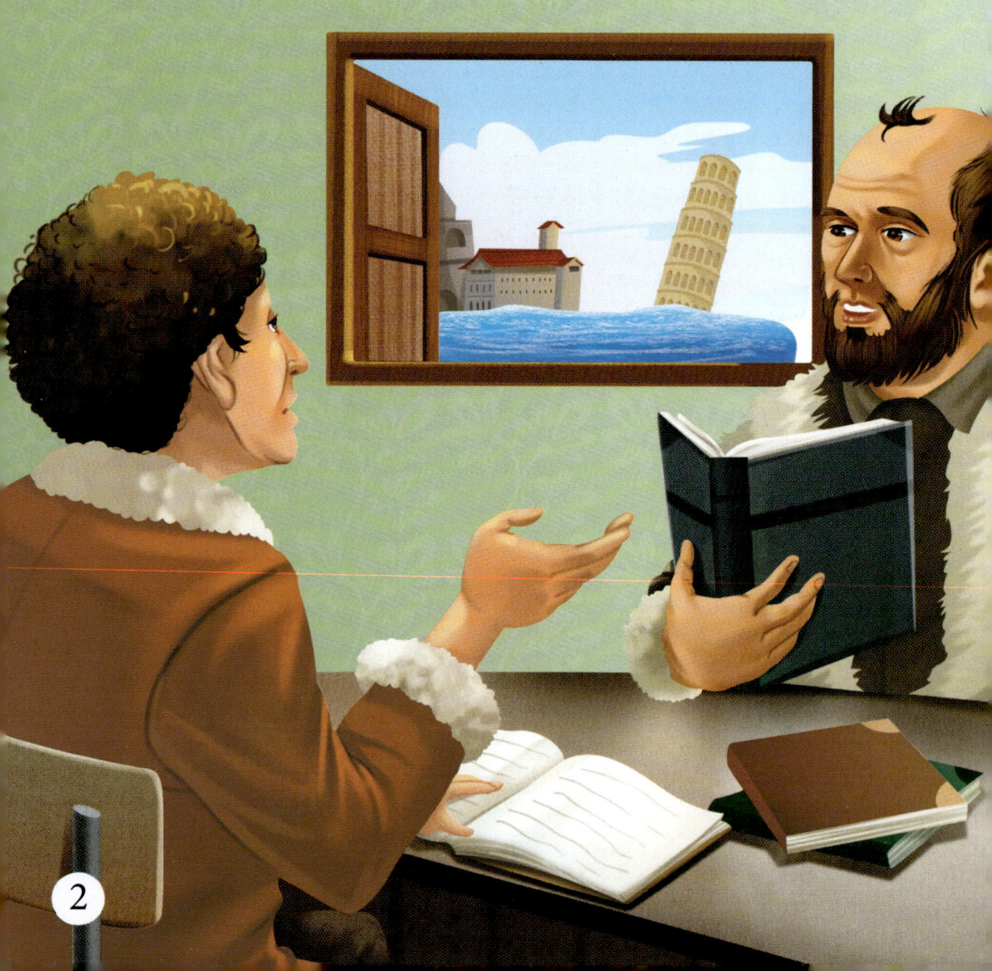

He started feeling more inclined towards natural philosophy. Then, when he had an opportunity to attend a lecture on geometry, he realised for sure that he was not really meant to study medicine!

But in those days, natural philosophy or geometry did not have prospects. Thus, convincing his father of this was a task! He still requested his father to allow him to pursue mathematics and natural philosophy.

His father reminded him that with mathematics, he would not be able to earn much.

"Father, I find mathematics more interesting than medicine!" Galileo pleaded.

His father consented reluctantly. And with this permission, Galileo's life changed!

He spent more time studying his preferred subjects, and in 1586, he published a booklet titled *The Little Balance* explaining the design of a hydrostatic balance he had invented.

Pondering more ideas, in 1593, he created a thermoscope based on a specific scientific principle. This instrument became the forerunner of the thermometer of the later generation.

In 1609, he improved upon the first practical telescope made by Hans Lippershey, with about 3x magnification and later 30x magnification. This came to be called the spyglass or the terrestrial telescope.

With that, he could see the magnified images on the Earth, the craters and lunar mountains on the Moon, the phases of Venus and even Jupiter's moons. In 1610, Galileo observed Saturn through his telescope, and in 1612, Neptune.

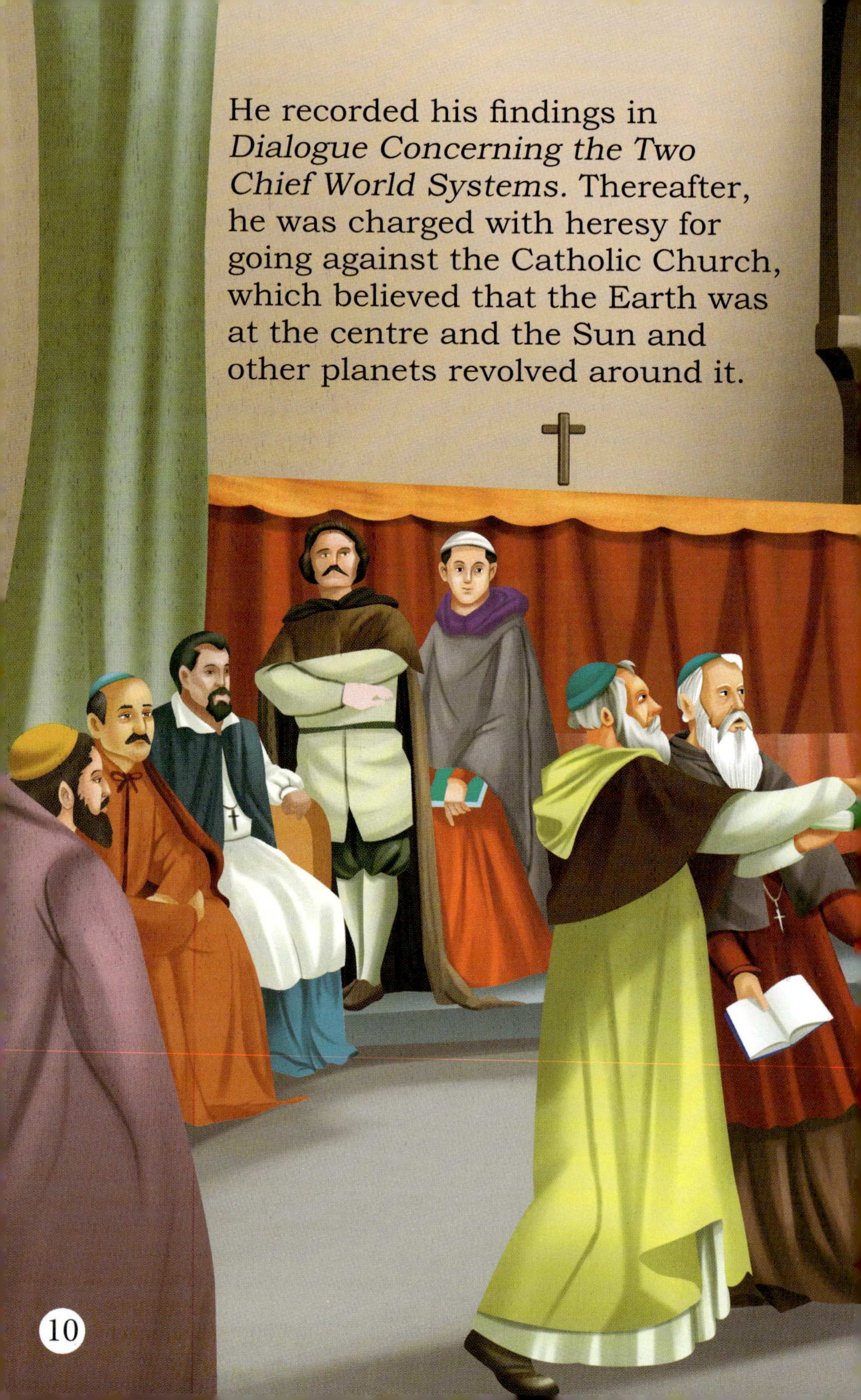

He recorded his findings in *Dialogue Concerning the Two Chief World Systems*. Thereafter, he was charged with heresy for going against the Catholic Church, which believed that the Earth was at the centre and the Sun and other planets revolved around it.

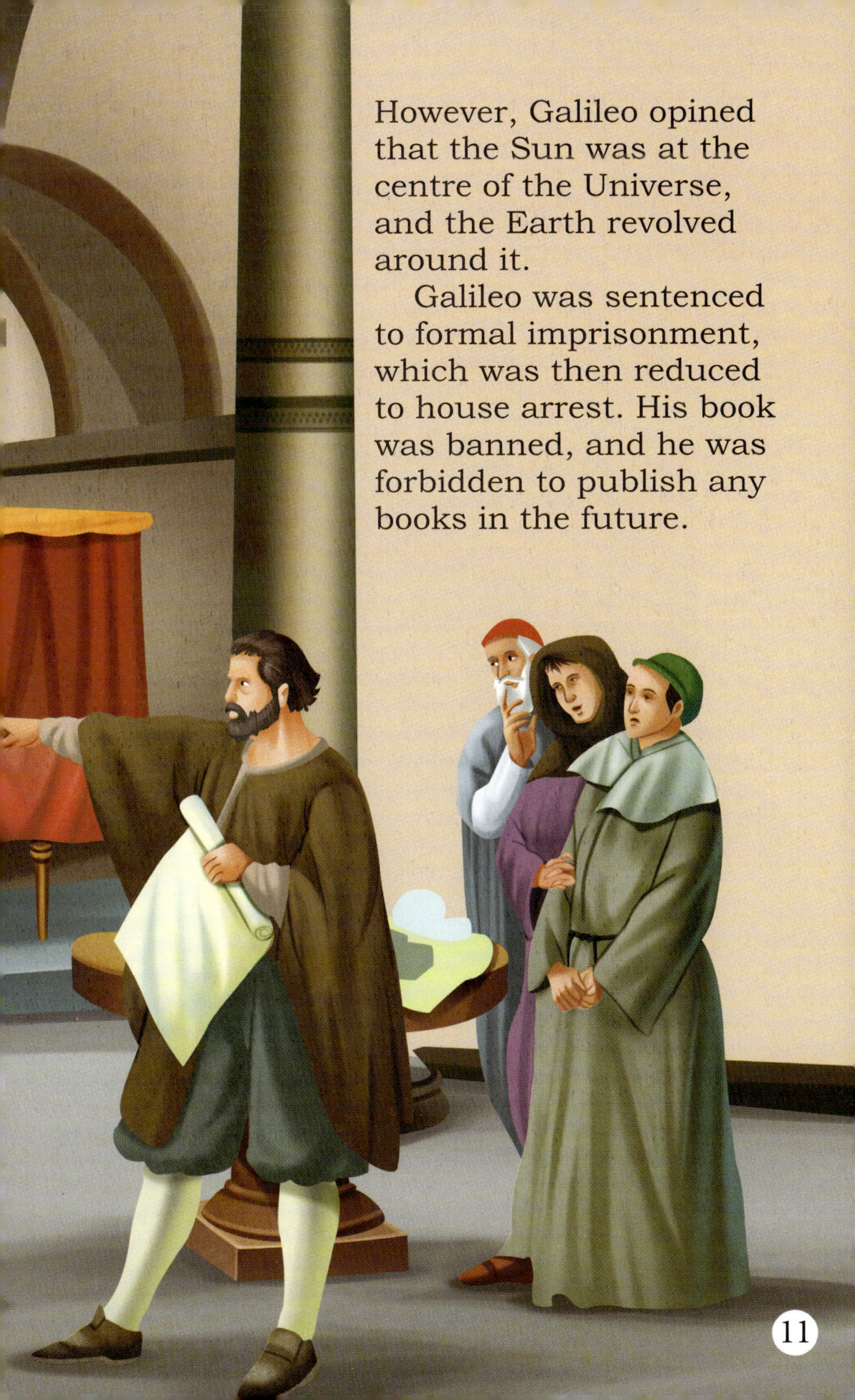

However, Galileo opined that the Sun was at the centre of the Universe, and the Earth revolved around it.

Galileo was sentenced to formal imprisonment, which was then reduced to house arrest. His book was banned, and he was forbidden to publish any books in the future.

Over the years, Galileo dwelt deep into science and astronomy, redesigning the basic telescope and studying the Universe at length! He studied velocity, gravity, speed, freefall and inertia and worked at length in applied science and technology.

Hailed as the "Father of Observational Astronomy," the "Father of Modern-Era Classical Physics" and the "Father of Modern Science" by Albert Einstein, Galileo died in 1642. With his death, the controversies surrounding him subsided. The ban on printing his works was lifted in 1718, and in 1741, almost a century after his death, Pope Benedict XIV authorised the publication of an edition of his complete scientific works.

Galileo left a trail of legacy for us to remember him forever. For example, the non-SI unit of acceleration, "Gal," is named after him. The four large moons of Jupiter he had discovered have been categorised as the "Galilean moons."

Then there is the concept of Galilean transformation, the Galileo Global Satellite Navigation System and the Galileo Spacecraft, the first spacecraft to enter the orbit around Jupiter—all named after him.

To top it all, the United Nations announced
2009 as the International Year of Astronomy
to commemorate the fourth centenary
of Galileo's first recorded astronomical
observations with the telescope!

GALILEO GALILEI

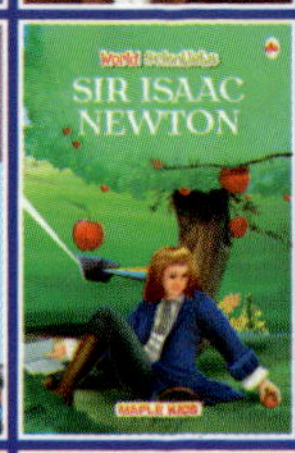

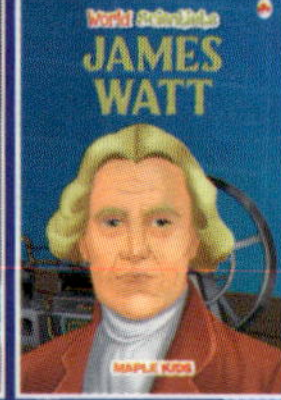

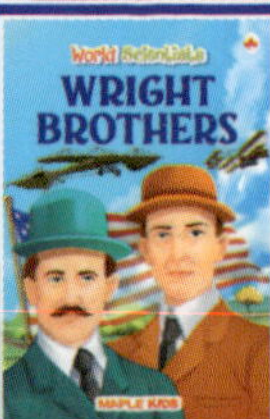

Sir Isaac Newton

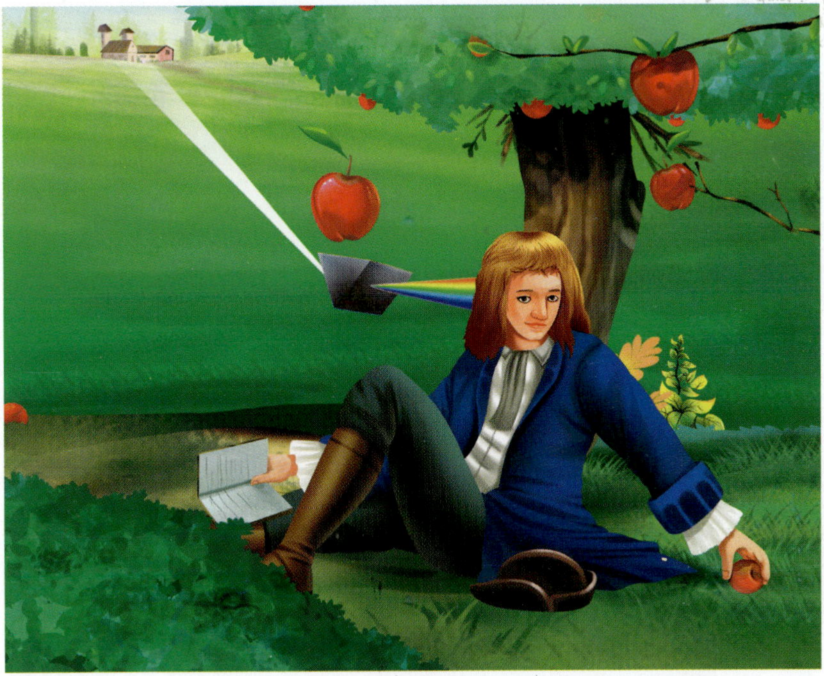

Published by

MAPLE PRESS PRIVATE LIMITED
Corporate & Editorial Office
A 63, Sector 58, Noida 201 301, U.P., India
phone: +91 120 455 3581, 455 3583
email: info@maplepress.co.in, website: www.maplepress.co.in

Printed in 2026
India

ISBN: 978-81-19898-11-4

23 22 21 20 19 18 17 16 15 14

Born in 1642 in Woolsthorpe, England, Isaac Newton's childhood was marked by hardships and family challenges. Raised by his mother after the death of his father, young Newton showed early signs of intellectual curiosity, experimenting with mechanical devices and displaying a keen interest in mathematics and science.

He began his formal education at the King's School in Grantham, England. While he wasn't interested in the traditional curriculum, his exceptional aptitude for mathematics and a knack for building mechanical contraptions became evident. Recognising his potential, his teacher persuaded Newton's mother to have him attend Trinity College, Cambridge, where he would go on to pursue his studies in mathematics and lay the foundation for his work in physics.

At Trinity College, Newton's intellectual prowess flourished as he delved into the rigorous academic environment, immersing himself in the study of mathematics and natural philosophy.

Under the guidance of Professor Isaac Barrow, he delved deeply into mathematics.

In 1665, the university temporarily closed down due to the bubonic plague epidemic. Newton then returned home and engaged in private study. Those were the years that he later called the "prime of my age for invention."

Around this time, one day, while Newton was sitting under an apple tree in a thoughtful mood, an apple suddenly fell right on his head. With a jerk, Newton looked up.

He stared at the apple and then at the branch above. He began to wonder why the apple fell down; why did it not fly up or fall sideways?

Then he looked up at the sky and thought of the Sun, the Moon and the stars. *Why don't the stars, the Moon and the Sun fall down on us?* he wondered.

Though this spark triggered his inquisitiveness to get deeper into this idea, it was only in 1687, when Newton was 44 years old, that it was conceptualised into the "Law of Gravitational Force."

Further to this, he also developed the three Laws of Motion, namely the Law of Inertia, the Law of Acceleration and the Law of Action and Reaction. He published these findings in his book, *The Mathematical Principles of Natural Philosophy.*

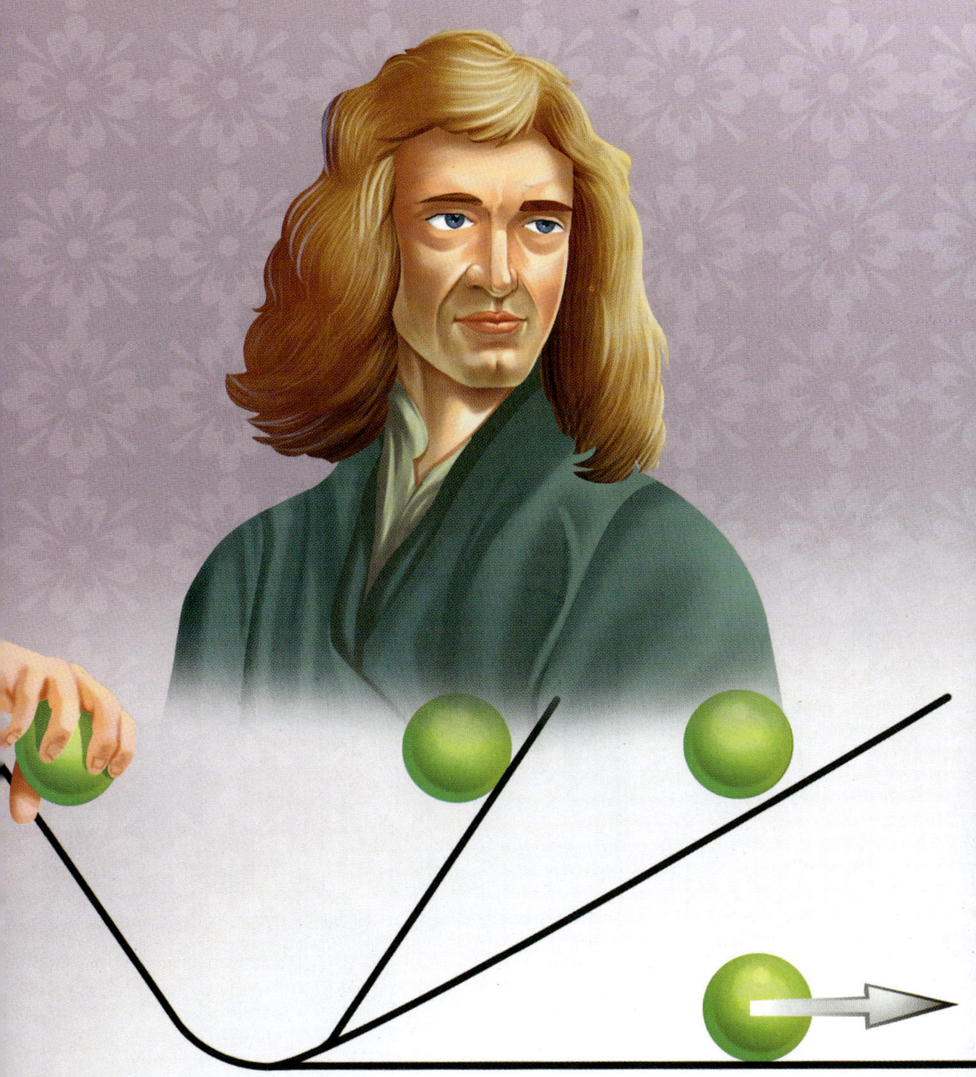

In the meantime, he returned to Cambridge in 1667 and served as a professor of mathematics and in other capacities until 1696.

He had also established himself as a great mathematician by developing concepts like calculus, differentiation and integration.

Simultaneously, Newton also explored "optics" and formulated several theories and concepts. In fact, he even designed the first known functional reflecting telescope, today known as the "Newtonian Telescope."

For that, he used mirrors in place of glass lenses, allowing the apparatus to focus on all the colours and give a more accurate image.

In his later years, Newton associated himself with politics and became a Member of Parliament for two brief terms.

Queen Anne honoured Newton with Knighthood in 1705, and he also served as "Warden" and "Master" of the Royal Mint as well as the President of the Royal Society.

Though Newton had expounded so many theories through his findings, it took time for the scientific community to accept them.

It was only when his successors like Charles Condamine and Pierre Maupertuis reassured his findings on the shape of the Earth as an "oblate spheroid" that European scientists were convinced that he was superior to his forerunners in the field.

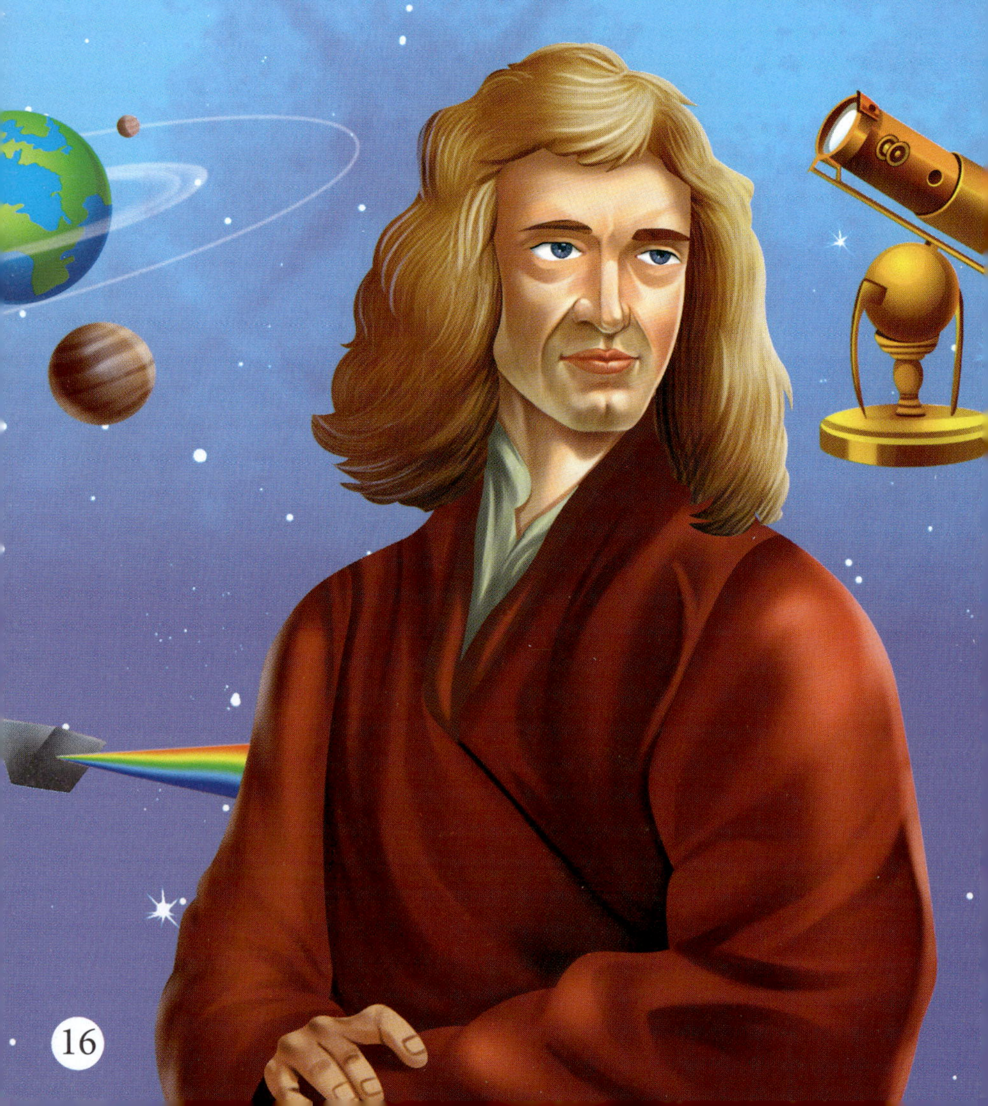

World Scientists

SIR ISAAC NEWTON

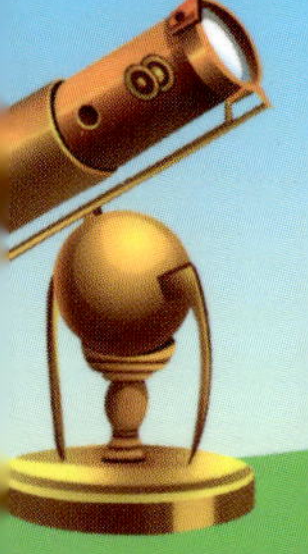

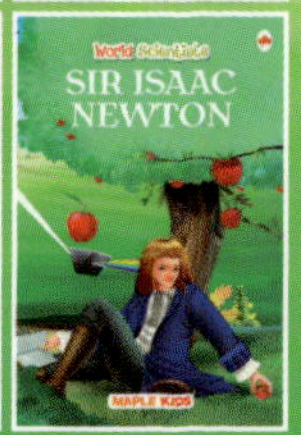

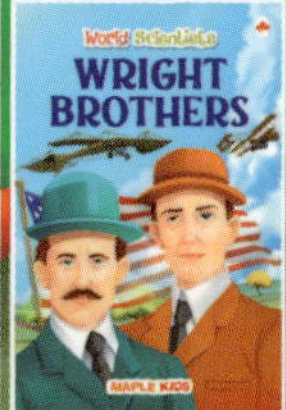

catalogue

e-book available

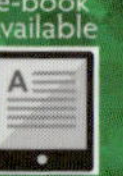

World Scientists
MARIE
CURIE
MAPLE KIDS

Marie Curie

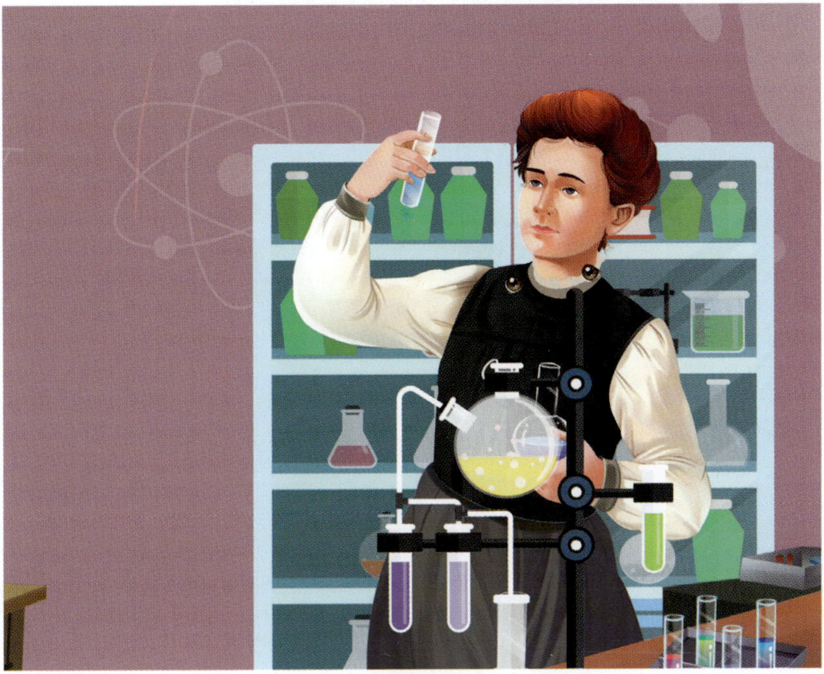

Published by

MAPLE PRESS PRIVATE LIMITED
Corporate & Editorial Office
A 63, Sector 58, Noida 201 301, U.P., India
phone: +91 120 455 3581, 455 3583
email: info@maplepress.co.in, website: www.maplepress.co.in

Printed in 2026
India

ISBN: 978-81-19898-21-3

23 22 21 20 19 18 17 16 15 14

Marie Curie was born as "Maria Sklodowska" in Poland on November 7, 1867. She inherited her science skills from her father, who taught mathematics and physics. From a young age, Marie was determined to become a scientist.

Marie started her career early. She became a tutor at the age of 17 and then a governess to financially support the education of her elder sister. During this time, she continued self-learning through reading books.

In 1890, she began her practical training in science at a chemical laboratory at the Museum of Industry and Agriculture near Warsaw's Old Town.

Finally, in late 1891, she left Poland to join the University of Paris to pursue her higher studies in physics, mathematics and chemistry. After earning her degrees, Marie stuck on to her scientific career when she met Pierre Curie. Their mutual interest in the natural sciences drew them closer, and they got married in 1895.

Marie was inspired by the discovery of a new phenomenon by Henri Becquerel in 1896, which referred to the radiance or light emitted by elements like uranium. She later called it radioactivity (active radiation).

Marie decided to pursue her doctorate on the same concept. She wanted to prove the presence of two more elements with powerful radioactivity, besides uranium, in the mineral ore, pitchblende.

Guided and supported by Pierre, Marie worked relentlessly. The couple's immense passion for the subject made them work even under poor lab arrangements and often in difficult conditions, both physically and financially. She soon discovered one element and called it "polonium" to show her patriotism for her mother country, Poland.

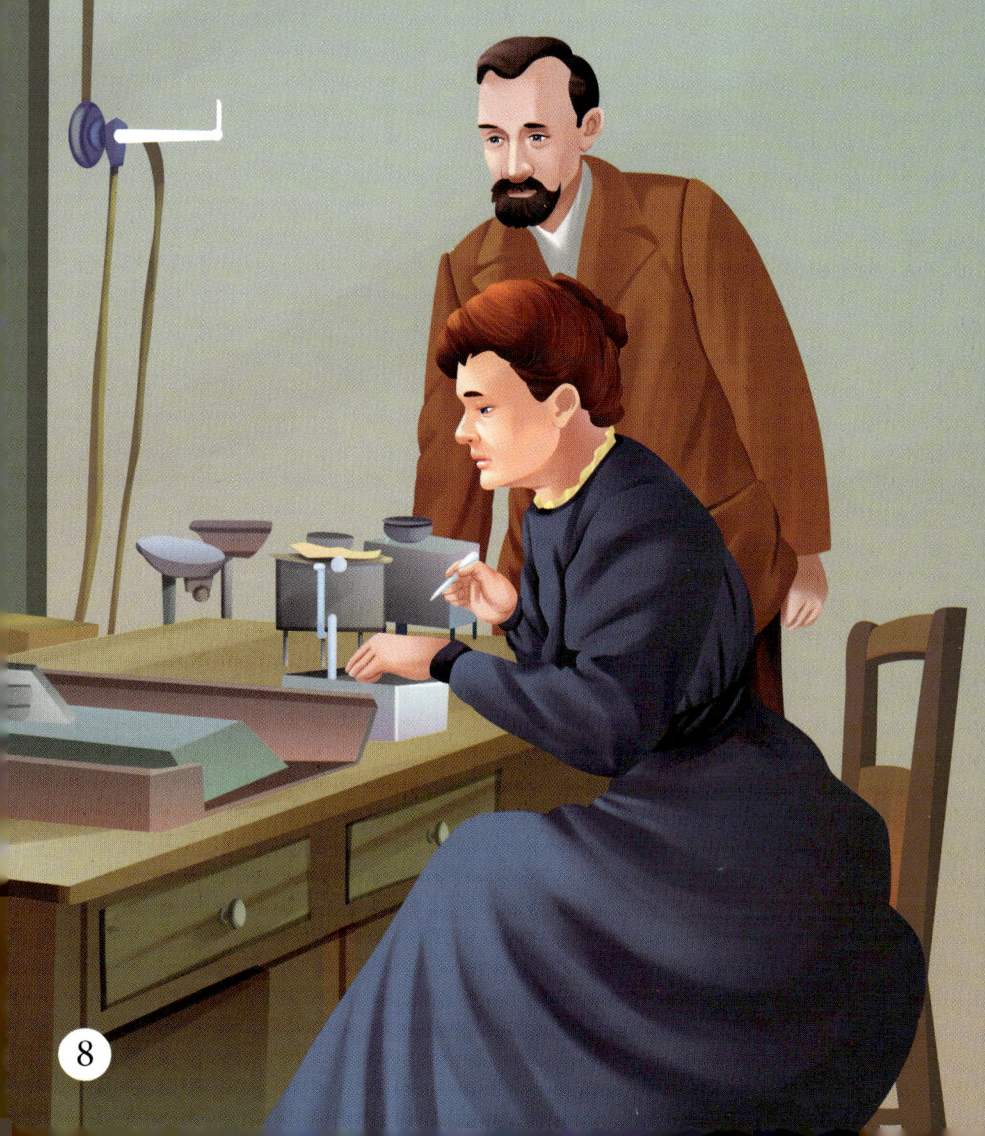

The couple continued their work, and on a fine night in 1902, they spotted the "spontaneously luminous" new substance with its phenomenal presence, which turned out to be more radioactive than polonium. They named it "radium."

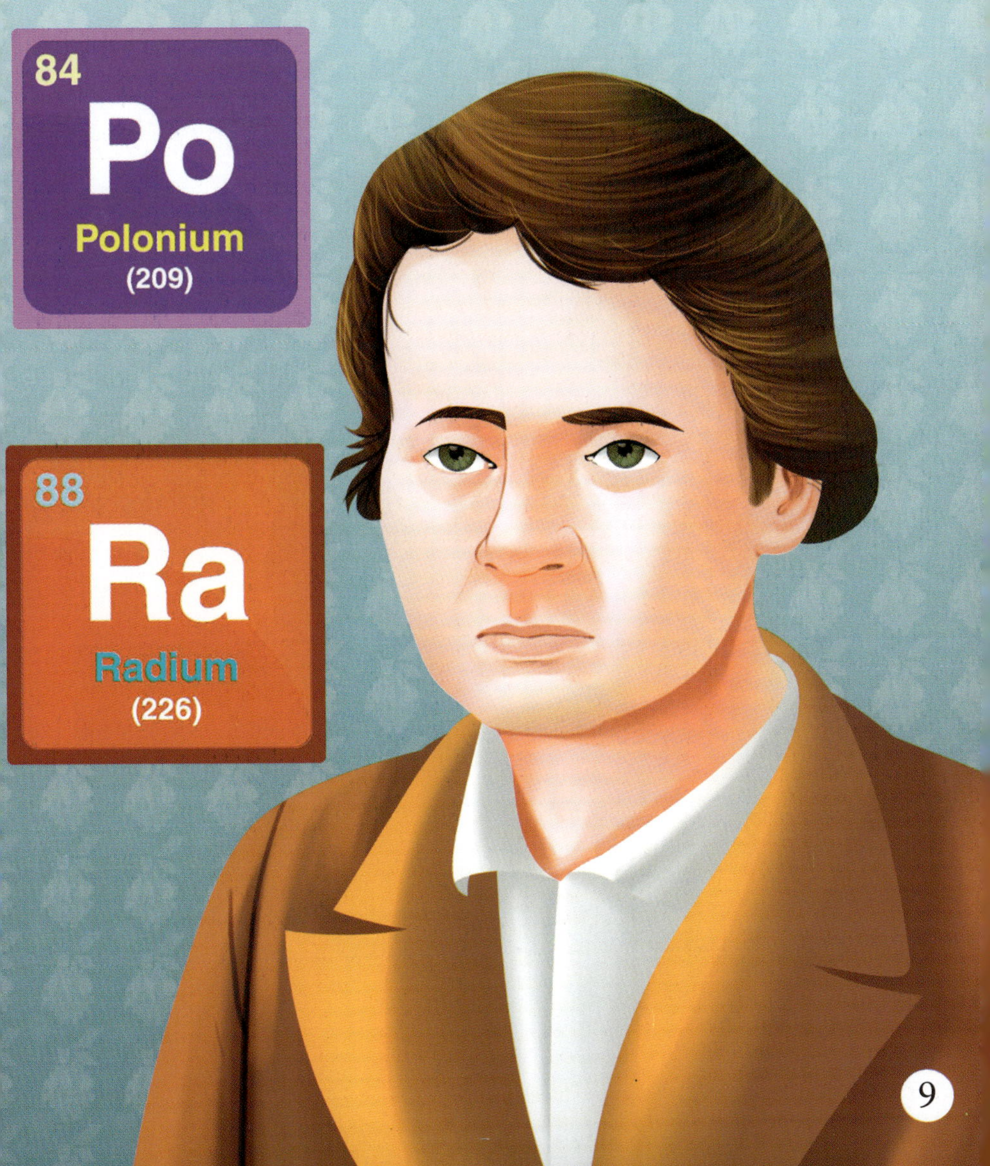

The discovery fetched the Curies the Nobel Prize in Physics in 1903.

The finding was a path-breaking achievement, as radioactivity enables accurate X-rays of the human body and is also a cure for cancer in the form of "radiation" treatment. It is called curietherapy, popularly known as radiotherapy.

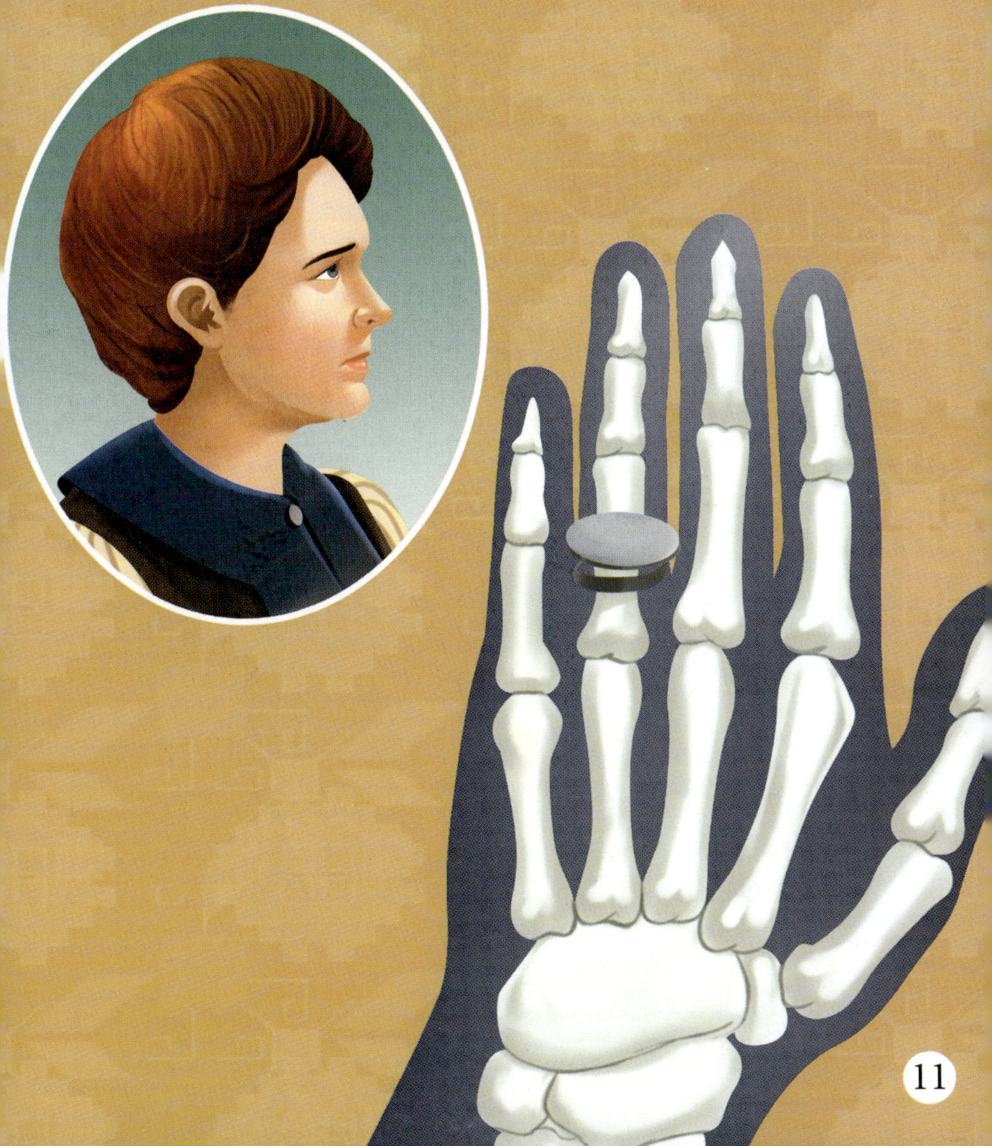

She then discovered the method of measuring radium by the rays it emitted. For which, she was awarded the second Nobel Prize, this time for chemistry, in 1911 and she became the first person to be awarded the prestigious prize twice!

Marie also developed a new unit of radioactivity, for which she gave the name "Curie" in memory of her late husband.

Pierre Curie

(1859-1906)

Marie's discovery of radiation was of great use during World War I, when mobile X-ray machines using radioactivity were driven to war hospitals in France and handled by women trained by Marie.

Known as Little Curies, the radiological cars helped doctors see broken bones and bullets inside wounded soldiers' bodies.

Marie Curie's discoveries are epoch-making, rewriting established ideas in the field of science and bringing in new hopes in medical science and defence.

Many of her papers are still to be brought to public attention as they are kept in lead-lined boxes due to their high levels of radioactive contamination.

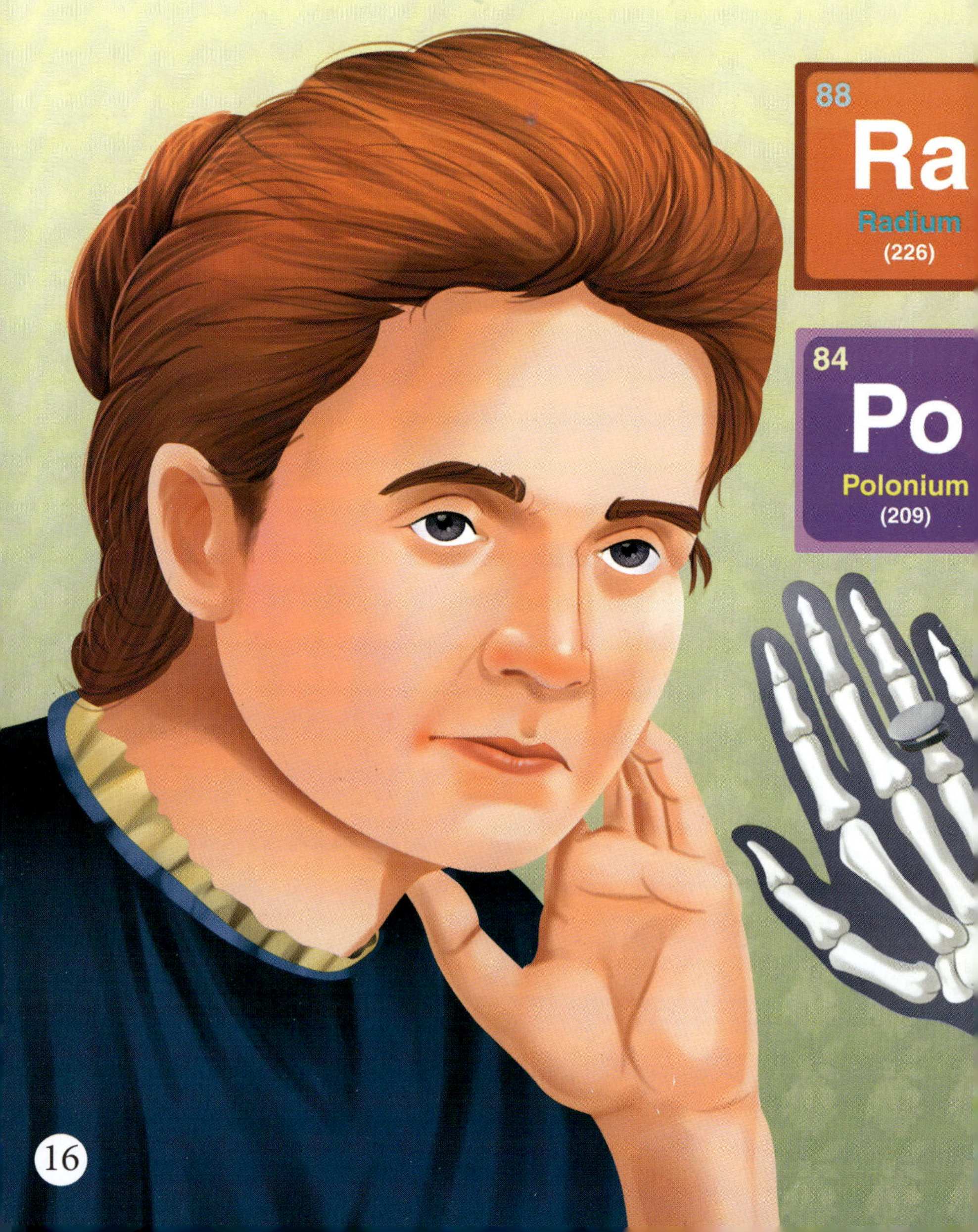

World Scientists

MARIE CURIE

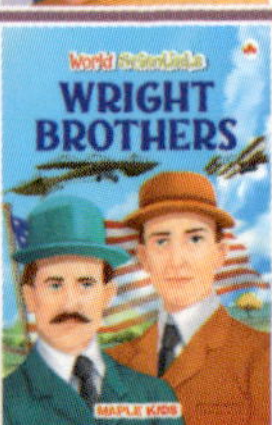

children

catalogue

e-book available

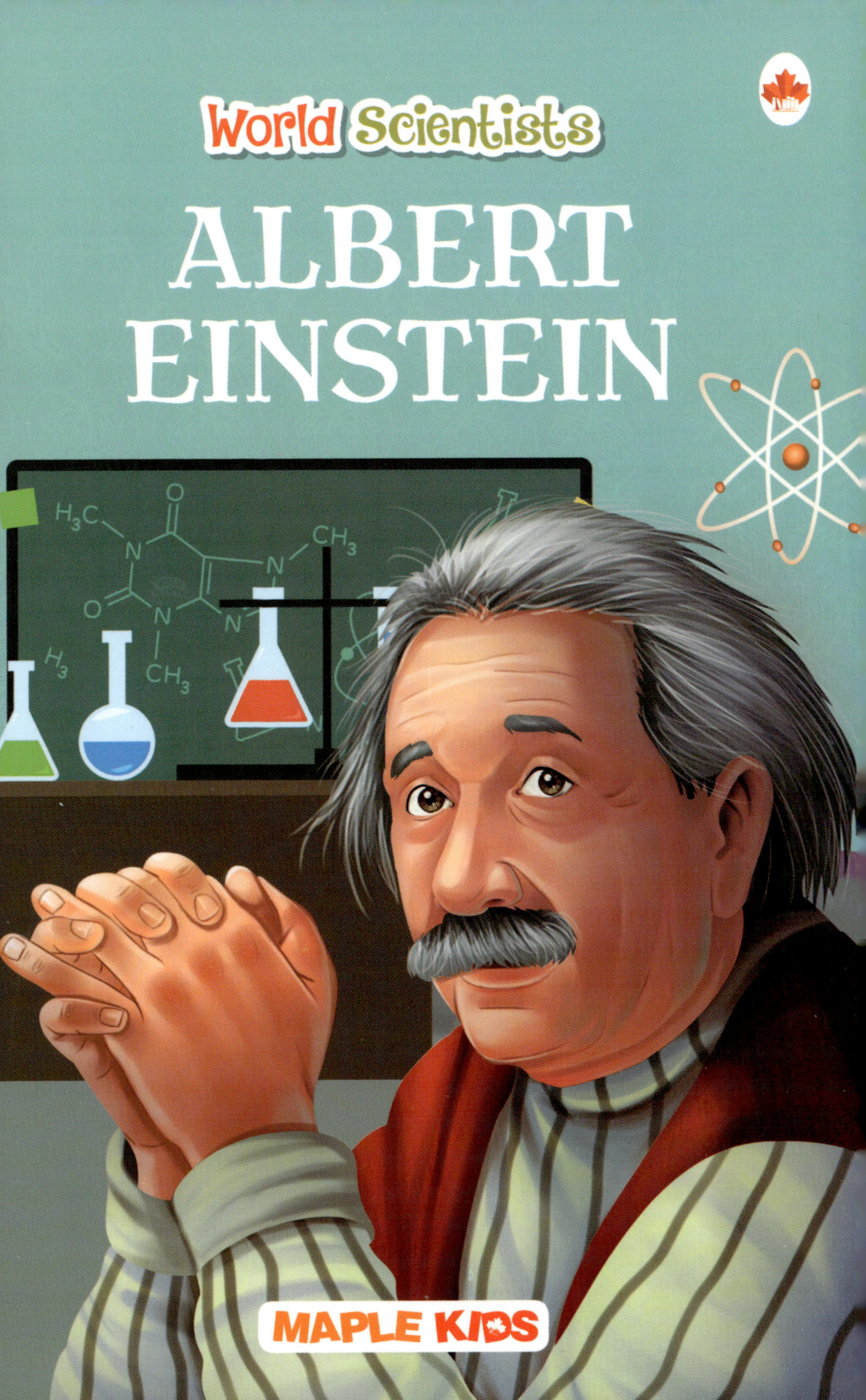

World Scientists
ALBERT EINSTEIN
MAPLE KIDS

Albert Einstein

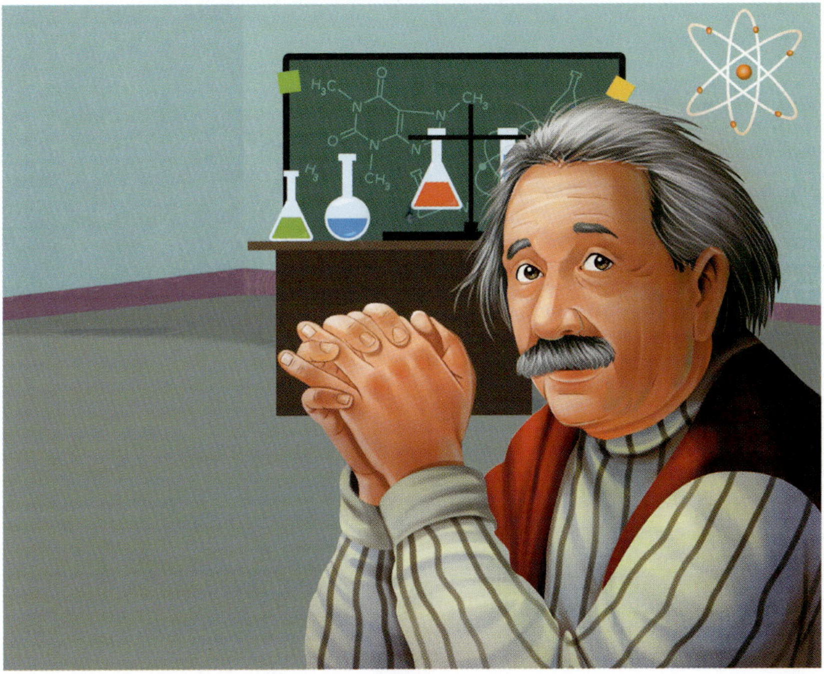

Published by

MAPLE PRESS PRIVATE LIMITED
Corporate & Editorial Office
A 63, Sector 58, Noida 201 301, U.P., India
phone: +91 120 455 3581, 455 3583
email: info@maplepress.co.in, website: www.maplepress.co.in

Printed in 2026
India
ISBN: 978-81-19898-52-7

23 22 21 20 19 18 17 16 15 14

"Albert, come here, quick..." Hermann Einstein called out to his four-year-old son.

The little boy ran up to his father, excited, and Hermann handed over a magnetic compass to him.

"Albert, look at this amazing thing… It's a gift for you!" Herman said to his son.

Little Albert received the gift and turned the compass around. His eyes widened with excitement when he found a needle in the compass pointing in just one direction, no matter which way he turned it.

"Father, this is amazing! I wonder how this little stick here (the needle) points back in the same direction every time!"

His father smiled and said, "That needle always points to the North."

"Hmm... but how?" murmured little Albert, already deep in thought.

"Father! I like this thing!" Albert said, happy with his acquisition. He ran off to play with the compass and find out the science behind it.

Little Albert's initial wonder about the compass needle left a deep impression on him. He was sure that there must be something "deeply hidden" behind things around him, as was the case of the compass, which always pointed to the North.

Though not very good at studies, Einstein excelled in mathematics and physics, thanks to his inclination and interest in these subjects. He became a self-learner, teaching himself complex mathematical concepts.

Around this time, he experienced a second "wonder" after reading a book on Euclidian plane geometry. He worked on proving the assertions and theorems given therein with absolute certainty.

Einstein's enthusiasm grew by leaps
and bounds over the years. The more he
read popular scientific books alongside
philosophical books, the more he was
convinced that many of the stories in the
Bible could not be true.

After his high school and secondary education in a polytechnic school, he worked as an examiner in the Swiss patent office in Bern. But in 1905, he came to a turning point in his life with the publication of five of his research papers.

Of these, his first paper, in which he proposed a model of intermolecular attraction, fetched him the doctorate (PhD) in 1905.

The other four papers, called the Annus Mirabilis papers, were indeed breakthroughs in the field of science, as they laid the foundation for modern physics, changing views on time, space and matter. These were the Photoelectric Effect, the Brownian Motion, his special Theory of Relativity and the equivalence of mass and energy.

Though his papers were initially ignored, they caught the attention of Max Planck, a great physicist of the time. His appreciation and confirmation of Einstein's ideas made him rise to popularity, and more and more offers for teaching came his way from prestigious institutions.

In 1907, Einstein achieved yet another milestone when he started reworking on the General Theory of Relativity. He formulated the equivalence principle for his new model of gravitation and used that principle to estimate the amount by which a ray of light from a star at a distance would be bent by the behaviour of the Sun as a gravitational lens.

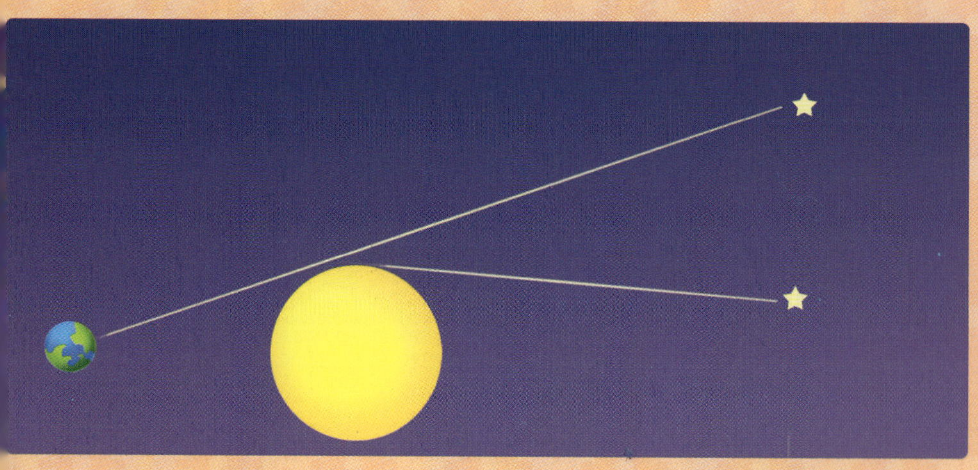

In 1915, Einstein completed his research, and on May 29, 1919, during a total eclipse of the Sun, his theory was put to the test, and the observations noted came out positive.

Einstein was acknowledged as a world-renowned physicist, the successor to Isaac Newton. The headline of The Times in London read: "Revolution in Science–New Theory of the Universe–Newton's Ideas Overthrown–Momentous Pronouncement–Space 'Warped.'"

In his later years, Einstein formulated equations that predicted that the universe is dynamic, which means it is either expanding or contracting. That came to be known as his "Theory of Cosmology."

For his immense contributions to theoretical physics and, in particular, for his discovery of the "Law of Photoelectric Effect," Einstein was awarded the Nobel Prize in Physics in 1921.

Even today, Einstein comes alive in front of us with his expressive face, his tongue sticking out and unkempt hair in any depiction of a "scientist" or in reference to an "absent-minded professor!"

That apart, he is still admired
universally, though his theories are
relevant and understandable only to the
"science community!"

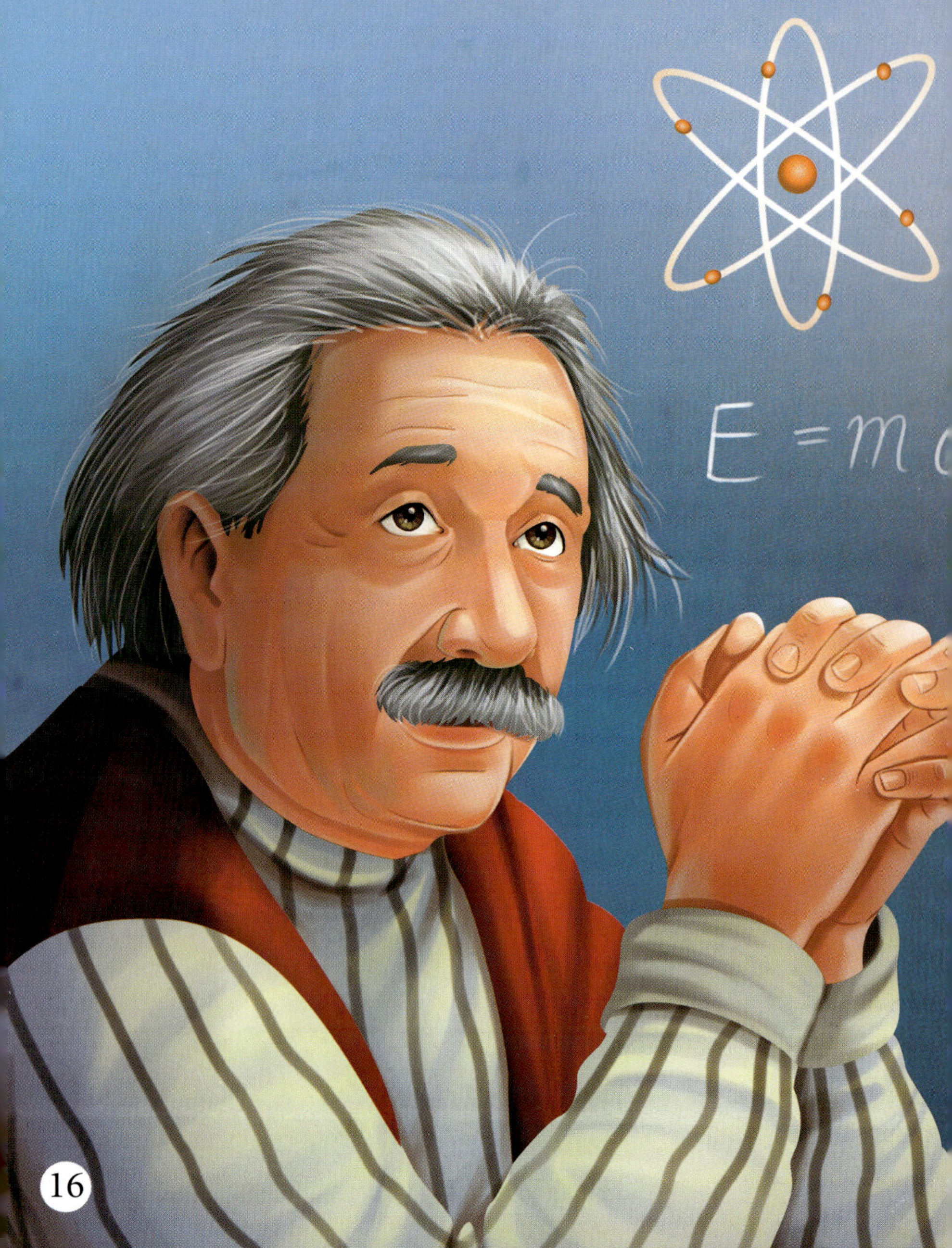

World Scientists

ALBERT EINSTEIN

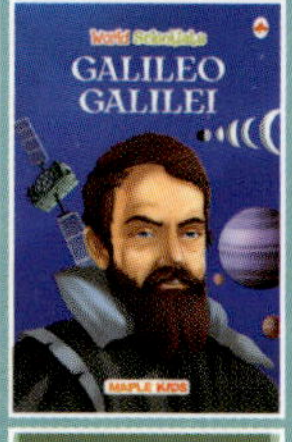

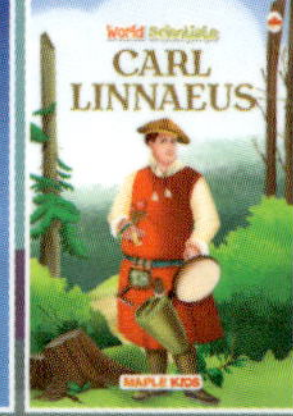

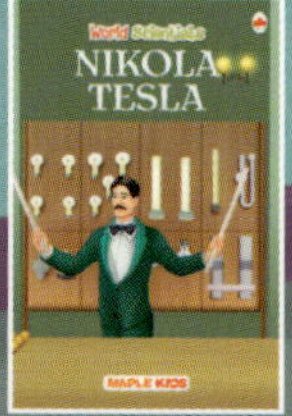

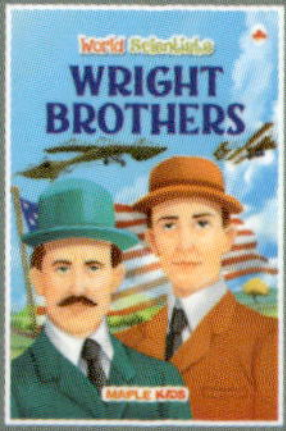

children

catalogue

e-book available

Indian Scientists

A. P. J. ABDUL KALAM

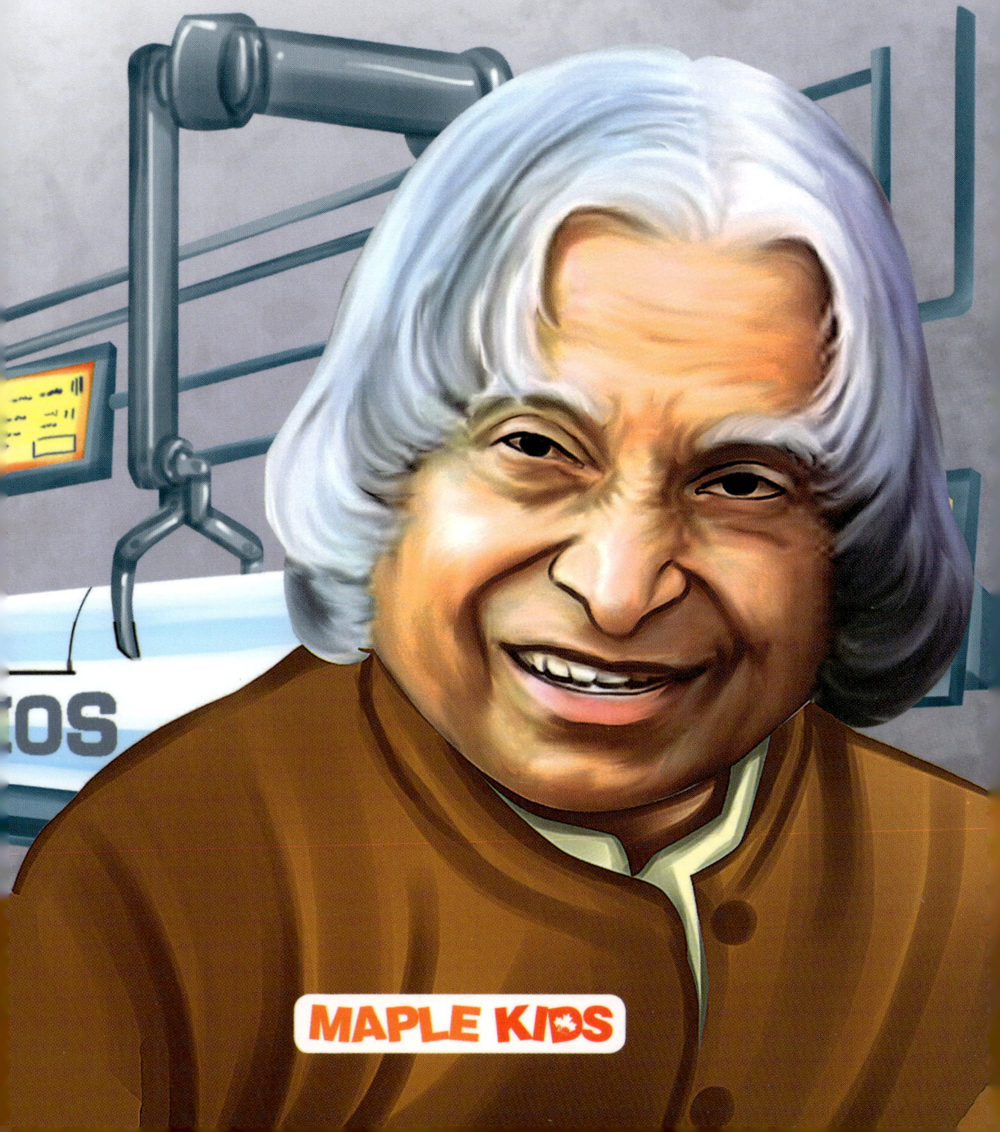

A. P. J. Abdul Kalam

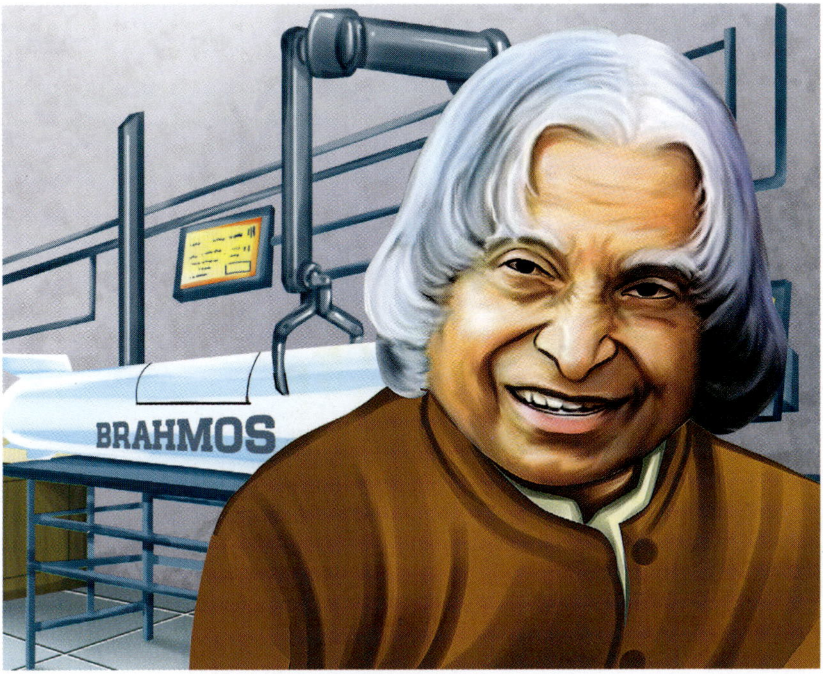

Published by

MAPLE PRESS PRIVATE LIMITED
Corporate & Editorial Office
A 63, Sector 58, Noida 201 301, U.P., India
phone: +91 120 455 3581, 455 3583
email: info@maplepress.co.in, website: www.maplepress.co.in

Printed in 2026
India

ISBN: 978-93-95976-84-8

32 31 30 29 28 27 26 25 24 23

Avul Pakir Jainulabdeen Abdul Kalam, popularly known as Dr. A. P. J. Abdul Kalam, was born in Rameswaram, Tamil Nadu.

He came from a wealthy family of boat owners who used to take devotees on their boats from Rameswaram to Dhanushkodi. However, after the Pamban Bridge was constructed, devotees didn't need a boat ride, which put Abdul's family out of business right before he was born.

Therefore, Abdul, his five elder siblings and his parents lived in a single room and faced extreme poverty. Seeing that it was difficult to even bring some food to the table, Abdul decided to sell newspapers at the age of eight to bring some money into the household.

3

Abdul also loved going to school and learning new things. Though he was quite an average student, he always gave his best efforts. His best friend, Ramanadha Shastry, was the son of the head priest. They went to the same school, sat together and studied together.

One day, a new teacher came to school and seeing Abdul sitting in the first row with the priest's son, he became furious.

"You!" he yelled, pointing to Abdul, who was wearing a skull cap. "You shouldn't be sitting beside the son of the head priest. Go, sit on the last bench!"

Abdul fearfully obeyed the teacher. Sitting on the last bench, he could see Ramanadha taking glances at him and weeping quietly. They told this incident to their respective fathers.

Both Abdul and Ramanadha's fathers were extremely upset by this and decided to confront the teacher. The teacher was called to the head priest's house, where Abdul's father and a Christian priest were also present with the kids.

"It isn't right to segregate on the grounds of religion," the head priest said calmly. "As a teacher, you're supposed to unite students, not divide them."

"Precisely," the Christian priest said.
"These are innocent children who look up
to you for guidance, and you must teach
them to be tolerant and loving towards
each other."

The teacher understood his mistake and embraced Abdul. "I'm sorry, Abdul. I shouldn't have treated you so badly."

That day, seeing the three wise men of different religions favouring peace over inequality, Abdul realised the power of unity.

Abdul completed his schooling at Schwartz Higher Secondary School before he moved to Madras to pursue his interest in Aerospace Engineering in 1955 at the Madras Institute of Technology. There, he faced immense pressure in academics but didn't stop working hard towards his dreams. He wanted to become a fighter pilot and even passed the exam. He secured the ninth rank but missed the opportunity because there were only eight seats available.

He graduated in 1960 and began working
at INCOSPAR, where he interned under
Dr. Vikram Sarabhai. Because of his hard
work and dedication, Abdul was transferred
to ISRO in 1969, where he became the
project director of SLV III, which was
India's first satellite launch vehicle.

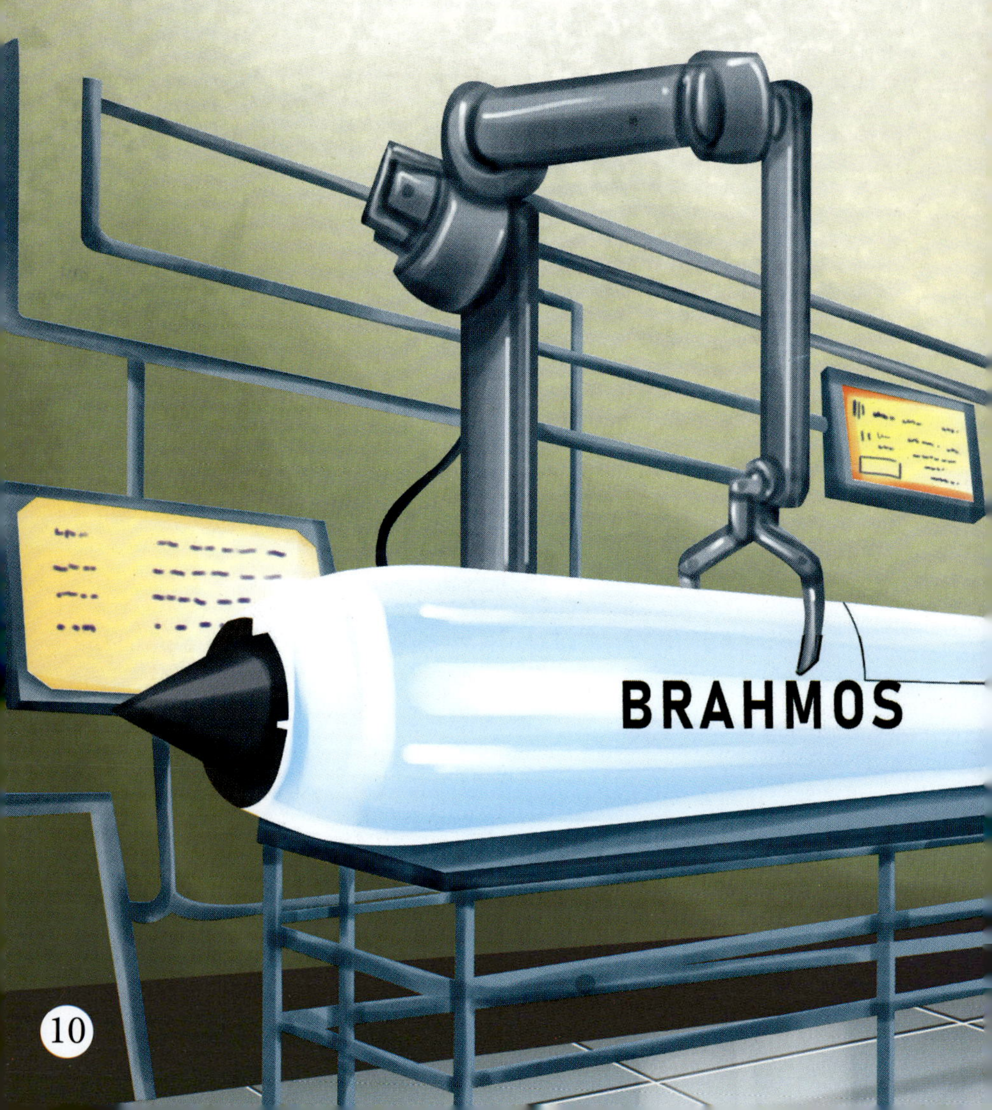

After ISRO, he joined DRDO, India's premier defence research organisation, where he spearheaded several projects for the creation of ballistic missiles.

He was the chief project coordinator
of Pokhran-II, India's nuclear test
programme in which 5 nuclear bomb test
explosions were conducted in May 1998.

In 2002, he was chosen to be India's 11th President. During his term, he focused on the welfare of the people and came to be known as the "People's President."

Dr. Kalam also contributed significantly to the medical field and helped design new prosthetics from space-age material; their weight came down to 400 grams! He said that it was one of the happiest moments of his life to see children running and cycling comfortably because of these space-age limbs.

In 2007, when his Presidential term ended, he became a visiting professor at several renowned educational institutions in India, including IIMs, IITs and IISc. He considered himself a teacher at heart and always gave some precious pieces of advice to students.

Dr. Kalam's contributions to developing military equipment, ballistic missiles and launch vehicle technology with the DRDO and the Indian civilian space programme earned him the title "The Missile Man of India." Billions of Indians still remember him as one of the best leaders they have seen.

Indian Scientists

A. P. J. ABDUL KALAM

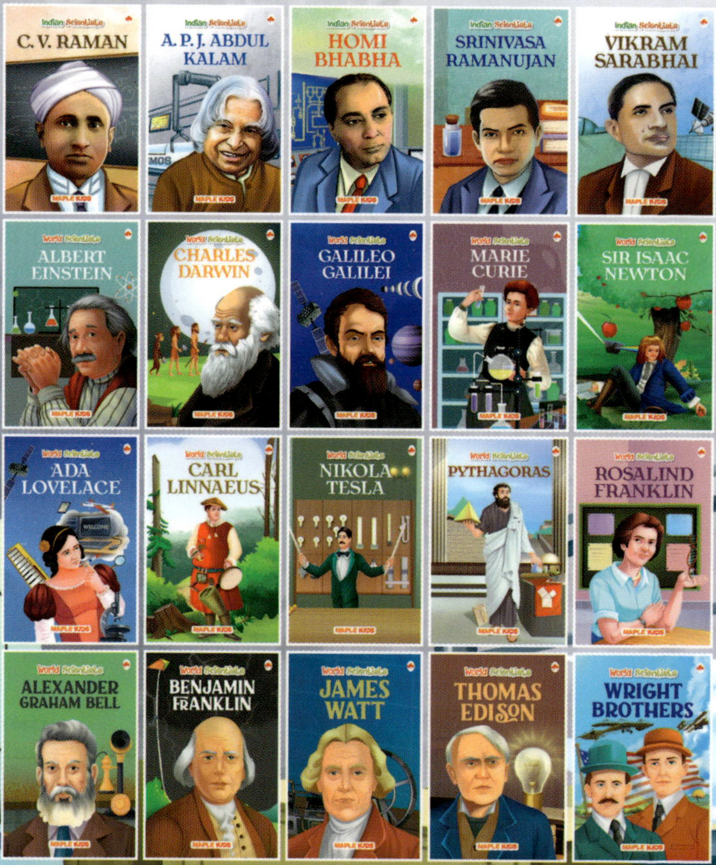

children

9 788119 898701

catalogue

e-book available

SRINIVASA RAMANUJAN

Srinivasa Ramanujan

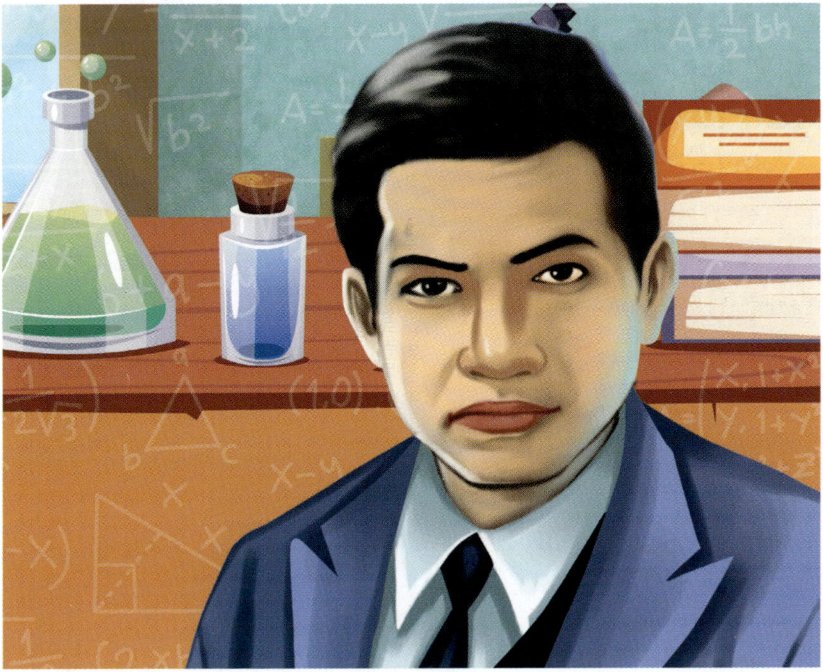

Published by

MAPLE PRESS PRIVATE LIMITED
Corporate & Editorial Office
A 63, Sector 58, Noida 201 301, U.P., India
phone: +91 120 455 3581, 455 3583
email: info@maplepress.co.in, website: www.maplepress.co.in

Printed in 2026
India

ISBN: 978-93-95976-98-5

32 31 30 29 28 27 26 25 24 23

Srinivasa Ramanujan was born in Erode, India. Among the five siblings, only his eldest brother lived long enough to enter adulthood, and everyone else had passed away at a very young age due to various illnesses.

Srinivasa's health was also affected by smallpox when he was two years old. He recovered, but his health always remained weak ever since.

At the time, India was ruled by the British, and they didn't provide good education to Indian children. All they taught were the basics, and wasn't of good quality. Due to this, Ramanujan found it too boring to attend school, and he started skipping classes.

One day, as usual, he had skipped school and was sitting under a tree. Suddenly, a police officer came walking towards him. He stopped and took him by the arm and started taking him along.

With wide eyes, a scared little Ramanujan asked, "Where are you taking me? What have I done?"

The police officer said, "I'm putting you in jail."

"Why! I promise I didn't do anything wrong!" Ramanujan cried.

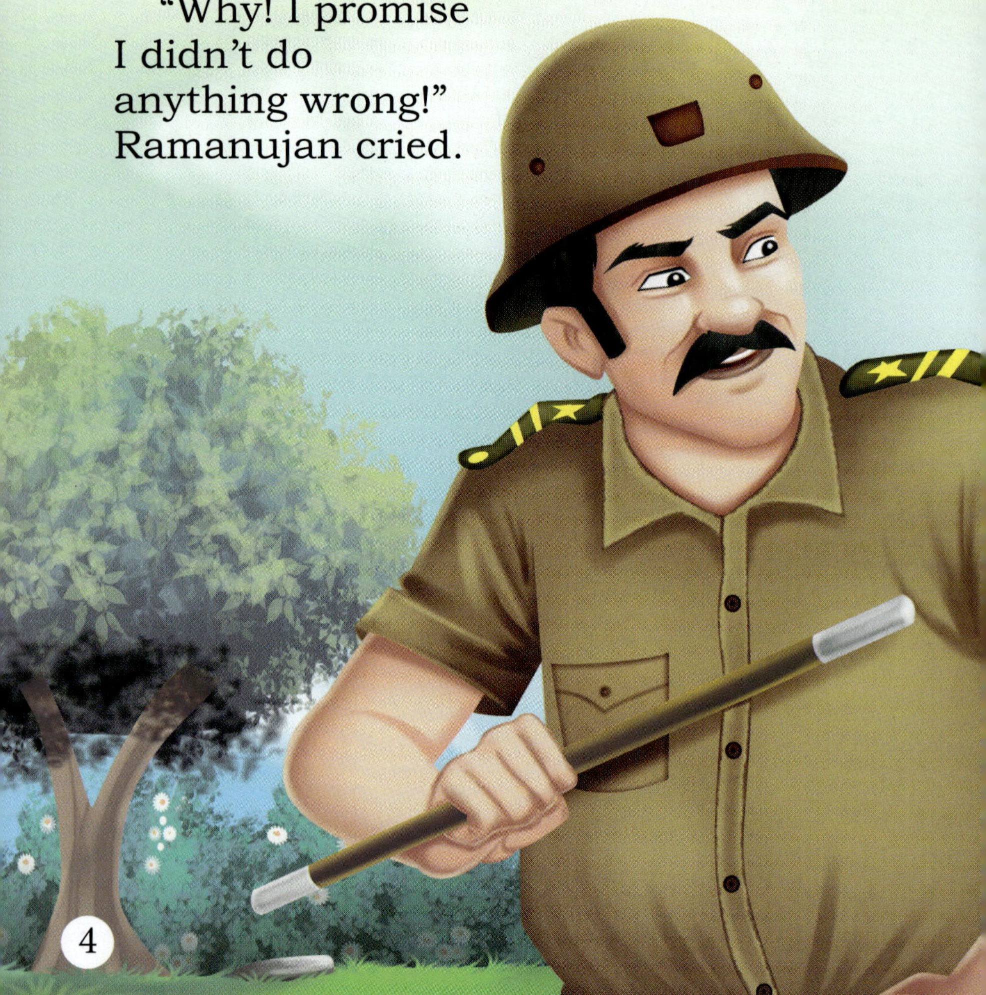

The police officer replied, "You don't think skipping school is wrong? If you don't want to go to school, then let's go to jail."

Hearing this, Ramanujan started crying louder. The officer looked back at the kid and felt bad for making him sob. He stopped in his tracks and tried to calm him down.

"Look," he said in a gentle voice, "to live in this world, you must have money. If you go to school, your education will help you get a job and earn money."

Ramanujan sniffled as he asked, "Were you going to put me in jail?"

The police officer laughed, "No. I was taking you to school. Your mother told me to look after you. She worries that if you don't learn, you won't earn. Do you understand me, son?"

Ramanujan nodded innocently and realised that the man was right.

From that day, he started attending school regularly even though he found it boring.

However, soon, he was introduced to a subject called Mathematics, and that suddenly tickled his interest in learning. Somehow, he seemed to enjoy Mathematics, and the concepts kept explaining themselves in his head before the teacher could even teach them.

One day, he got his hands on a book written by Mathematician G. S. Carr called *A Synopsis of Elementary Results*. It was approximately a thousand pages long and contained nothing but plain theorems without any explanations. The more Ramanujan read this book, the more he understood every equation better.

It was as if his brain magically knew the outcomes of every formula and equation.

He secured brilliant grades in high school and got a scholarship to attend college.

Here, too, he excelled in Mathematics and left his professors in awe of his abilities. But since he was deeply inclined to only one subject, he ended up failing in every other subject.

Without a college degree, Ramanujan couldn't secure a job as well.

Instead of feeling disappointed, he focused on his mathematical research and found it fulfilling.

But being an independent researcher didn't earn him a wage. He started applying for jobs everywhere and soon secured a position as a clerk at the port of Madras in Tamil Nadu, earning thirty rupees per month.

He found the work easy and hence finished it all quickly so that he could work on his theorems. His superiors noticed his abilities and found them so exceptional that they suggested he write letters to professors in England.

Taking their advice, he drafted a letter to Professor Godfrey Hardy at Cambridge University.

Upon receiving such a long letter from an Indian stranger, Hardy thought he was being fooled. But when he read the eleven pages of theorems that Ramanujan had attached with the letter, he was astonished.

He immediately wrote back and invited Ramanujan to England, promising to take care of his expenses.

In 1914, Ramanujan arrived in England and started his research with a team of mathematicians.

His methods were different, but they realised that he was an absolute genius. When they asked him how he taught himself the subject and could create such complex equations, he said, "An

equation for me has no meaning unless it represents a thought of God. I think of Goddess Mahalaxmi and Narasimha, and then, scrolls of equations just make themselves visible to me."

In his short life of 32 years, Ramanujan drafted approximately 3,900 theorems, and most of them were proven right. One of them was used to explain the black holes 92 years after his death, proving that Srinivasa Ramanujan was not just a gifted genius but also way ahead of his time.

Indian Scientists

SRINIVASA RAMANUJAN

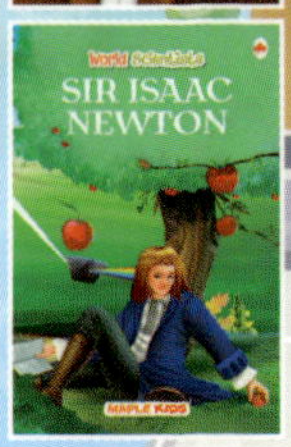

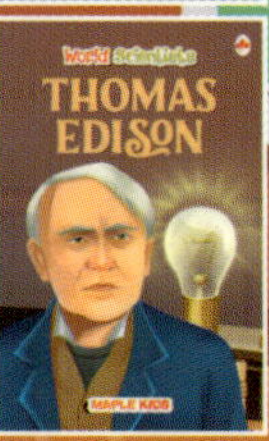

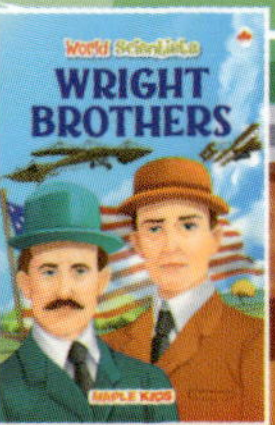

children

Indian Scientists
HOMI
BHABHA
MAPLE KIDS

Homi Bhabha

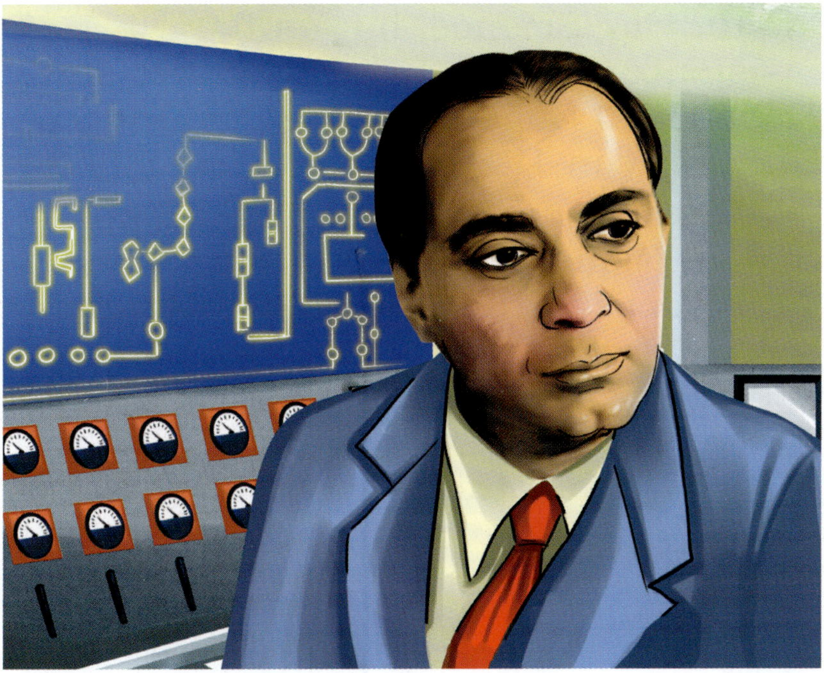

Published by

MAPLE PRESS PRIVATE LIMITED
Corporate & Editorial Office
A 63, Sector 58, Noida 201 301, U.P., India
phone: +91 120 455 3581, 455 3583
email: info@maplepress.co.in, website: www.maplepress.co.in

Printed in 2026
India

ISBN: 978-93-95976-97-8

32 31 30 29 28 27 26 25 24 23

Homi Jehangir Bhabha was born in 1909 into a wealthy Parsi family in Bombay. Homi was a bright student interested in studying Science, but on the insistence of his father, he went to study Mechanical Engineering at Cambridge University in 1927.

Even his uncle, Dorabji Tata, supported this decision as he wanted Homi to join Tata Steel after his graduation. However, soon after entering college, Homi realised that he wanted to study Physics and wrote a letter to his father wherein he said,

I seriously say to you that business or a job as an engineer is not the thing for me. It is totally foreign to my nature and radically opposed to my temperament and opinions. Physics is my line. I know I shall do great things here. For, each man can do best and excel in only that thing of which he is passionately fond, in which he believes, as I do, that he can do it, that he is born and destined to do it.

His father understood his desire and didn't object to his decisions thereon. Thus, Homi finally redirected his career and dedicated himself to Physics. He was particularly drawn to the concept of cosmic rays and earned his PhD for his thesis on the "Absorption of Cosmic Radiation" in 1934.

For his work on Compton and Bhabha Scattering, he gained recognition not just among his peers but several other scientists associated with Cambridge University, including Niels Bohr.

In 1939, he returned to India for his annual vacation, but because of the Second World War, he couldn't go back.

During this time, Homi was offered the position of a reader in Physics at the Indian Institute of Science, Bangalore, which was headed by the Nobel Laureate C. V. Raman. Homi accepted this position and started conducting his research on cosmic radiation.

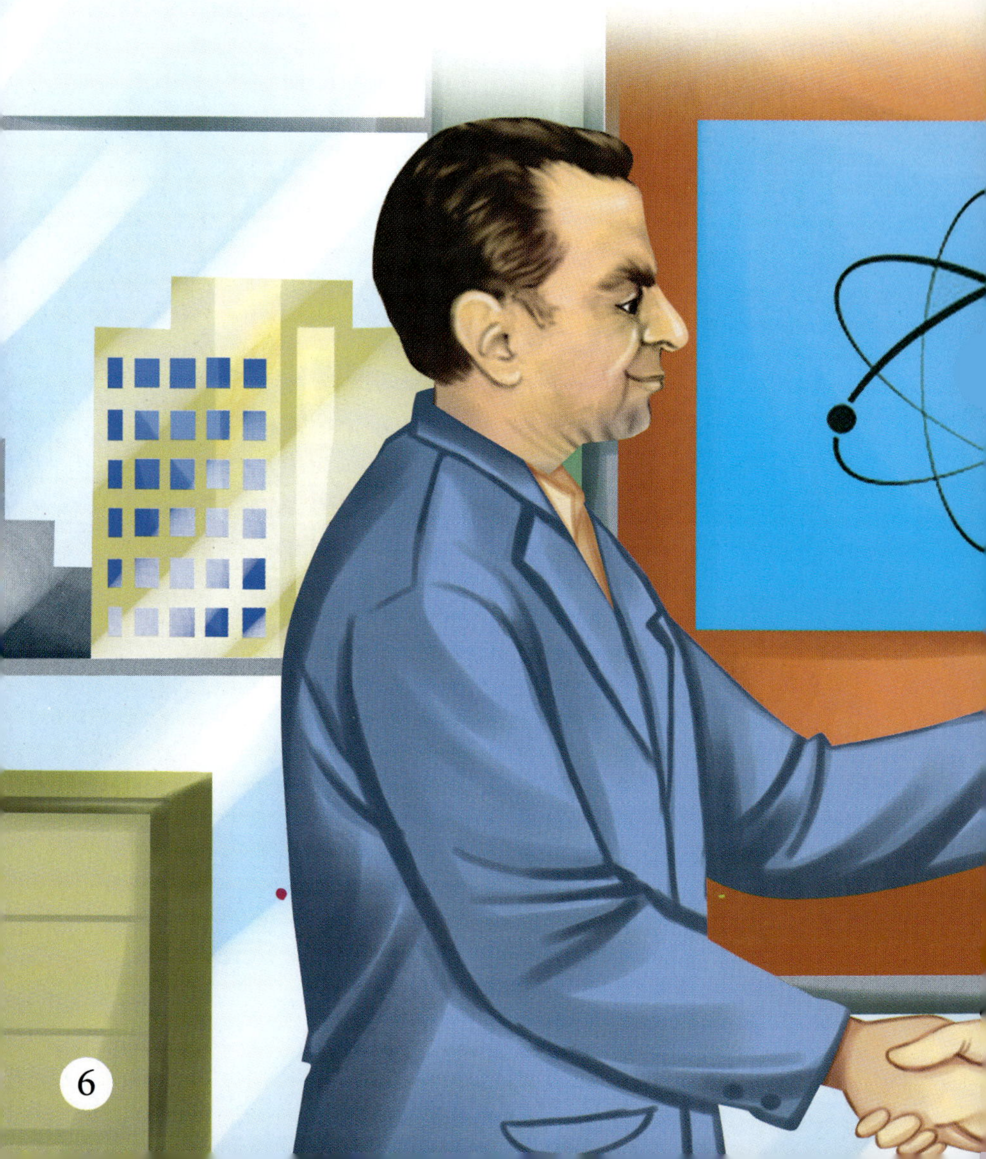

Two years later, he met Vikram Sarabhai, who also came to the institute because he couldn't complete his master's due to the war. Homi recognised his potential and made him an assistant in his research. Soon, they became very close friends.

Once, Dr. Bhabha tried to convince Jawaharlal Nehru to take a step in the direction of nuclear programming.

"If we have nuclear power supporting us, our nation would be empowered and secured amid any adversity," Dr. Bhabha said.

Nehru replied, "But our concerns at the moment are rooted in the development of industries, society and the overall betterment of people. How is atomic energy going to solve these issues on the ground level?"

"I understand, but this can be worked upon simultaneously. I'm thinking decades ahead from now; atomic energy would play an important part in the economy and the industry of countries," Dr. Bhabha argued.

"We've been a peaceful nation, Homi. Wouldn't such a venture paint us in the light of violence as it could potentially be used in the bomb?" Nehru questioned.

"Then, we make it clear that atomic power can also be used to maintain the peace of the world," Homi replied.

While this discussion was adjourned for
a while, Dr. Bhabha approached
J. R. D. Tata and proposed the same idea
to them. J. R. D. Tata agreed with his
ideology and funded the establishment
of the Tata Institute of Fundamental
Research in 1945.

The same year, the Atomic Energy
Establishment was also inaugurated in
Trombay, which is today known as the
Bhabha Atomic Research Centre. Dr.
Bhabha also erected the Atomic Energy
Commission, where he became the first
Chairman and worked with Sarabhai
closely on their various projects.

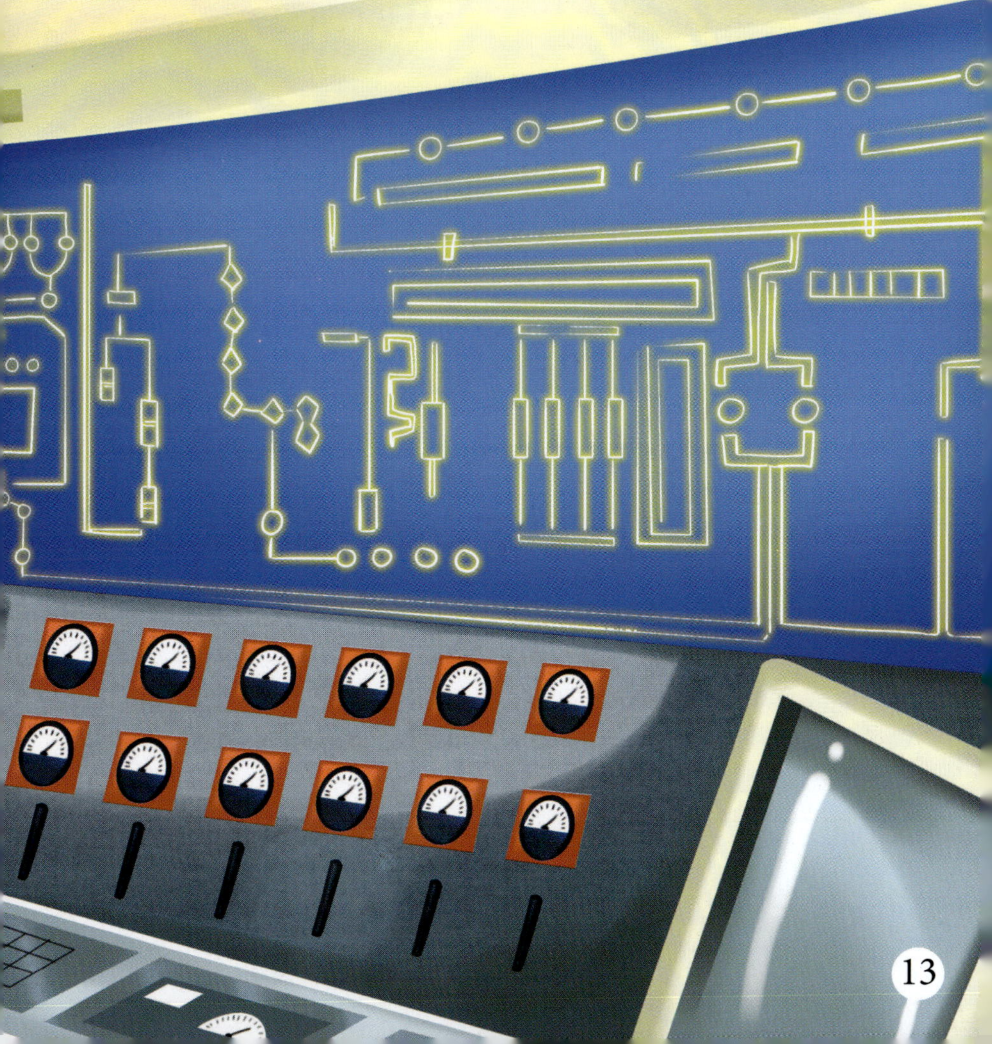

In the 1960s, Dr. Bhabha began
to urge the government to give
a green flag for commencing
with the nuclear
programmes, and it was
finally approved.

However, in 1966, when Dr. Bhabha was flying to Vienna for the International Atomic Energy Agency, his flight plummeted near Mont Blanc in France, and India lost a great scientist in that unfortunate accident.

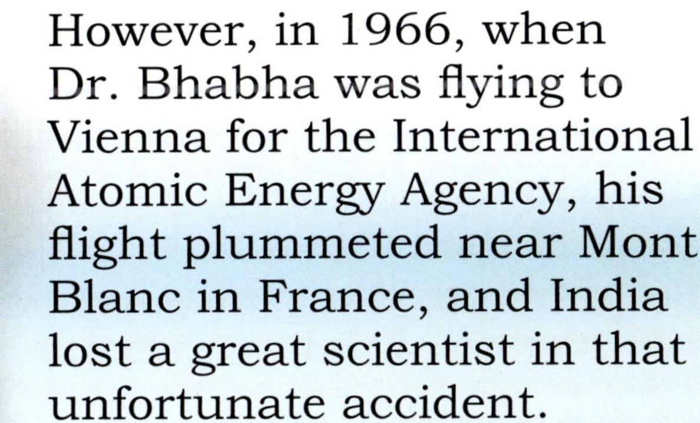

All his life, Dr. Homi Bhabha was determined to use his knowledge for the betterment of his country, and he lived up to it till his last breath. Such was the story of the Father of the Indian Nuclear Programme, who continues to live in every atom of India's success.

Indian Scientists

HOMI BHABHA

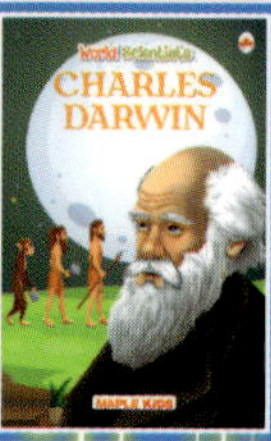

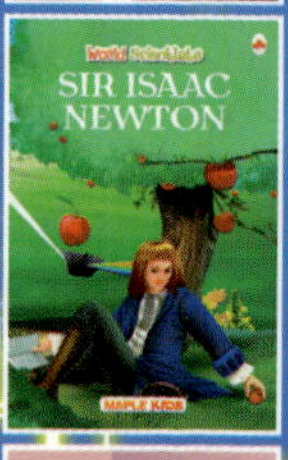

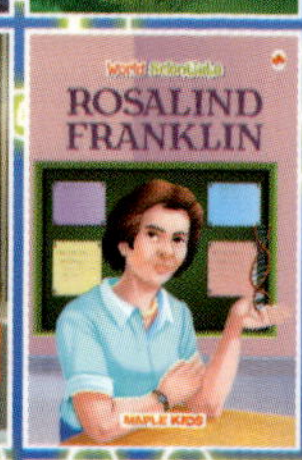

VIKRAM SARABHAI

Vikram Sarabhai

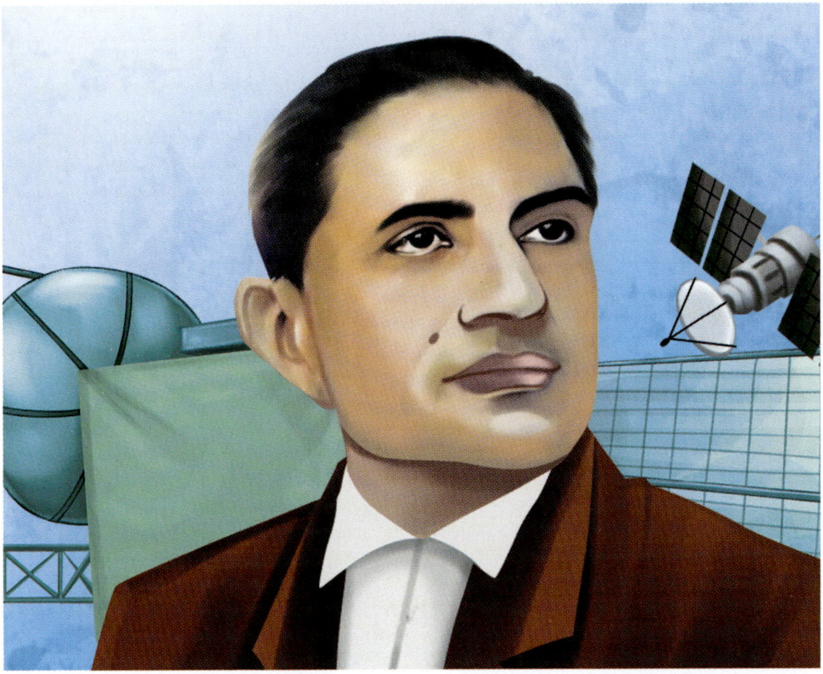

Published by

MAPLE PRESS PRIVATE LIMITED
Corporate & Editorial Office
A 63, Sector 58, Noida 201 301, U.P., India
phone: +91 120 455 3581, 455 3583
email: info@maplepress.co.in, website: www.maplepress.co.in

Printed in 2026
India

ISBN: 978-93-95976-79-4

32 31 30 29 28 27 26 25 24 23

Dr. Vikram Sarabhai was born in 1919 in Ahmedabad. He was the son of Ambalal Sarabhai, one of India's most renowned industrialists at the time. This background offered a comfortable environment for Vikram to grow up in.

Since his family was also dedicated to the Indian Independence Movement, he, too, learnt to love his country and wished to do something for the nation one day.

Vikram was a sharp student with a strong memory. When he reached high school, he found himself falling in love with Science. He was constantly fascinated by the laws of Physics and was especially mystified by space.

Initially, he joined Gujarat College in Ahmedabad but found that the resources available at Cambridge University were much more suitable for his endeavours. His thirst for knowledge motivated him to attend college abroad. Since money was never a problem and his father wanted to offer the best of everything to his son, Vikram flew to England and picked Natural Science as his major.

He had the best time learning from some
of the most renowned professors and
studying in an environment favourable
for honing the best scientists. Though
the pressure of the curriculum was quite
heavy, Vikram didn't mind it and found
himself feeling more dedicated towards his
dreams. He was so quick at understanding
concepts and simplifying them for his
peers that they often joked about how
Vikram should be the professor. And
every time, he would humbly say, "No, no,
there's so much left for me to learn."

However, in 1939, the Second World War broke out, and the conditions in England didn't seem safe anymore. As a result, with a heavy heart, Vikram returned to India but found that the atmosphere in India was also deep in conflict.

"What's the matter, Vikram? Are you not happy being back home?" his father Ambalal asked Vikram one day.

Vikram said, "No, Baba. I feel like I decided to come back too soon. Here, the atmosphere isn't suitable for my studies."

"What do you mean?" his father asked.

"I was there learning from some highly qualified professors. Besides, the war would end sooner or later. Perhaps I could've just stayed," Vikram explained sadly.

"Conflict is always going to be a part of our lives, son. Whether it's external or internal, the key is to try and overcome it with what's available to us." He then handed Vikram a letter written by the Indian Nobel Laureate, C. V. Raman.

"C. V. Raman?" Vikram asked, reading the letter which stated that he had been accepted for an interview at the Indian Institute of Science in Bangalore to continue his research. He was so happy that he hugged his father and asked how it had happened.

"I sent them your research papers, and they found some potential in you," he shrugged.

"Thank you so much, Baba. I won't disappoint you," Vikram said.

"Do your best for the nation," Vikram.

Thus began the next chapter of Vikram's life when he met C. V. Raman, the Director of IISc at the time. He was also introduced to Dr. Homi Bhabha, who took a liking to Vikram's curious intelligence and brought him on board his research on cosmic rays. They worked day and night at the Cosmic Ray Unit and conducted several experiments.

Vikram found that IISc was giving him more satisfaction than Cambridge University. In 1947, he earned his PhD for his thesis on "Cosmic Ray Investigations in Tropical Latitudes" and founded the Physical Research Laboratory, which became the first significant pillar of space science in India.

Vikram's fascination for space only kept intensifying over the years. After India gained independence, he insisted that the Indian Government launch an organisation that specifically dealt with astrophysics. He convinced Prime Minister Jawaharlal Nehru that such a body would act as a catalyst in India's overall development.

Thus, the Indian Space Research Organisation (ISRO) was established in Bangalore in 1969, and Vikram Sarabhai was made the Chairman.

Vikram, along with other scientists at ISRO, went on to pioneer the creation of Aryabhata, India's first satellite.

It was because of him that India's
potential in space research gained light.
He was awarded the Padma Vibhushan
for his life's work.

Vikram believed that a scientist's work should make the lives of the common people better, and he dedicated himself to that cause. Till today, he continues to inspire scientists to keep unravelling the mysteries of the universe for the betterment of mankind.

Indian Scientists

VIKRAM SARABHAI

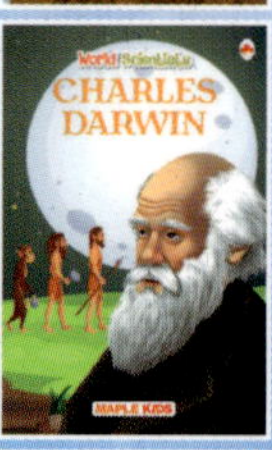

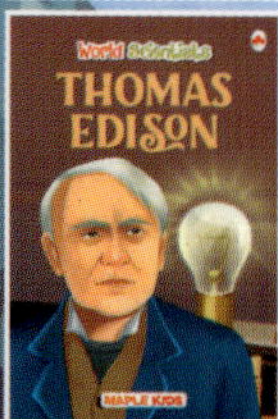

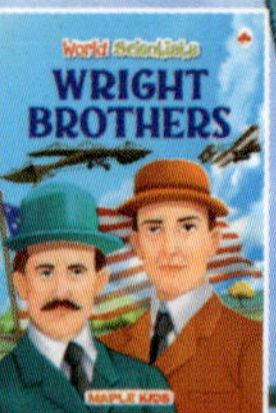

children

catalogue

e-book available

">